Rita

Hope you enjoy reading
this.

M Dragnel 13 April 2016

My Triumph over Prejudice

MY TRIUMPH OVER PREJUDICE

Martha Wyatt-Rossignol

A MEMOIR

University Press of Mississippi Jackson

Willie Morris Books in Memoir and Biography

www.upress.state.ms.us
The University Press of Mississippi is a member
of the Association of American University Presses.
All images courtesy the author.

Library of Congress Cataloging-in-Publication Data

Names: Wyatt-Rossignol, Martha, author.
Title: My triumph over prejudice / Martha Wyatt-Rossignol.
Description: Jackson : University Press of Mississippi, 2016. | Series:
Willie Morris Books in Memoir and Biography | Includes bibliographical
references and index.
Identifiers: LCCN 2015032209 (print) | LCCN 2016000140 (ebook) | ISBN
9781496806031 (hardback) | ISBN 9781496806048 (ebook)
Subjects: LCSH: Wyatt-Rossignol, Martha. | African
Americans—Mississippi—Fayette—Biography. | African Americans—Civil
rights—Mississippi—History—20th century. | Race
discrimination—Mississippi—History—20th century. | School
integration--Mississippi—Fayette. | Mississippi—Race
relations—History—20th century. | Interracial marriage—Mississippi. |
Fayette (Miss.)—Biography. | BISAC: BIOGRAPHY & AUTOBIOGRAPHY /
Cultural
Heritage. | SOCIAL SCIENCE / Discrimination & Race Relations. | HISTORY /
United States / State & Local / South (AL, AR, FL, GA, KY, LA, MS, NC, SC,
TN, VA, WV).
Classification: LCC E185.93.M6 W93 2016 (print) | LCC E185.93.M6 (ebook) |
DDC 305.896/07307620830904--dc23
LC record available at http://lccn.loc.gov/2015032209
British Library Cataloging-in-Publication Data available

Contents

Acknowledgments   vi

1   Growing-up Years   3

2   The Awakening of Fayette   25

3   First Marriage   55

4   Joe Rossignol's Trip to Mississippi   80

5   The Deterioration of Marriage   96

6   The Divorce   116

7   My Marriage to Joe   131

8   New Start   150

9   The Boycott   167

10   The Election   186

11   My Children's Problems Dealing with an
Interracial Marriage   197

12   Hello, Bermuda . . . Goodbye, Racism   213

Acknowledgments

I want to thank my husband and soul mate of forty-plus years, Joseph A. Rossignol, for all of his patience and understanding while I pursued this dream of putting my life's story into a book. Many times over, he read and reread my unfinished manuscript and helped me with the endless hours of research. I want to thank my dear friend Claudine Middleton for believing my life was worthy of a book and for giving me the idea to write about it; Jean Stoess of Reno, Nevada, for all the typing and editing she performed over a five-year period and for believing in me and my work; Walt Harrington, author of *Crossings: A White Man's Journey into Black America*, for pointing me in the direction of University Press of Mississippi for publication. I also want to thank my family and dear friends and I give them a heartfelt "thank you" for all their wonderful words of encouragement so that this manuscript could reach its potential. After years of writing and rewriting, I finally found the perfect editor to help me get it all together—thank you, Linda Cashdan.

My Triumph over Prejudice

Figure 1. Martha and her sister

1
Growing-up Years

Fayette, Mississippi, my hometown, is located about seventy-five miles southwest of Jackson, not far from the Mississippi/Louisiana border. The little town, with its surrounding rural communities, is nestled between Natchez and Vicksburg, two old historic steamboat ports on the Mississippi River. When I was growing up there in the 1950s, the population of Fayette was less than two thousand residents, and it hasn't increased much since.

Both the town and the surrounding area were named for eminent political figures during the early nineteenth century, when the population consisted primarily of many slaves and their few masters. Jefferson County, then a collection of plantations and smaller farms, was named after our country's third president, who had also been a slaveholder. Fayette was named after the honorary citizen and supporter of American independence, Gilbert du Motier, the Marquis de La Fayette, who was taking a farewell tour of the region in the 1820s when the town was settled.

Even now, the downtown area has only two major thoroughfares, Main and Poindexter Streets, which cross at the very center of town. During my youth, a few ancient brick commercial buildings still existed, such as Freeman's Department Store and the Guilminot Hotel, both dating back to the early 1800s. The Guilminot Hotel was then the only three-story building in downtown Fayette.

At the head of Poindexter Street stood the Jefferson

County Courthouse, another old brick commercial building, where the lobby held an antique Coke machine and a WPA (Works Progress Administration) forestry display. Across from the courthouse was the Confederate Memorial Park, which could only be used by white people. The park's single monument was a statue of a Confederate soldier leaning on his rifle. During the warm months, older white people sat on benches in the park or milled around on the lush green grass under the big shade trees scattered throughout. During the cold months, the park remained deserted except for that lone stone soldier.

On its face, Fayette was a charming hamlet in a pretty part of the state. Fine old elms, pecans, magnolias, and beeches shaded the streets. The trees seemed to have held the same air captive among them for so long that they had acquired their own unique atmosphere. Like many southern towns, Fayette was quiet and peaceful and, during my early years, about as segregated as a town could be. I could clearly see that blacks were the majority, but it seemed as if blacks knew their place and the whites knew theirs, and no one crossed those invisible lines.

In the white section of town, the stately homes had remained unaltered for so many decades that they seemed frozen in time, throwbacks from another era. The homes had yards of beautiful flowers with well-manicured lawns, all maintained by black hands. What were known as the black neighborhoods, however, were situated in downtown Fayette across the tracks. The proverbial railroad tracks separated the two regions.

To visit a black family who lived downtown, one had to pass through the pristine white neighborhoods, with their rich foliage and cement sidewalks. Once a person was across the dividing line, the difference was literally like night and day.

Sometimes it seemed that the only inhabitants of the black neighborhoods were small children and old people, all sitting outside in the sweltering heat of summer evenings while the young adult workforce toiled across the tracks, and the rest found other places to entertain themselves. The homes varied in quality, from broken-down shacks with no running water to moderately nice-looking wood-framed ones. The beat-up old shacks undeniably predominated, and since there was no indoor plumbing, that meant many smelly outhouses. There were no paved streets or sidewalks in the black neighborhoods; the roads were all dirt or all gravel, or sometimes both, but the dust was forever flying free. In my memory, I can still feel the heat and dust clinging to my body and still smell those smelly old outhouses.

My brothers and sisters and I did not live in the black section of town, but in a rural area outside Fayette, a world far removed from the happenings of the town, a country-side consisting of woodlands and farmlands with all kinds of wildlife running free. About a third of all black residents in Mississippi, like our family, were engaged in farming. Some families had their own farms to live on, but there were quite a few, like us, who sharecropped. This was a system where a landowner allowed a tenant to use the land in return for a share of the profits. My father farmed cotton, corn, and sugarcane. When the cotton was harvested, it was taken to the gin to be sold and the profits were used to pay off the landlord. Profits from the corn and sugarcane were used to pay off debts as well. My father made molasses from the sugarcane and sometimes cans of molasses were given in lieu of money.

In February 1950, when I was five months old, our mother, Verine Sanders Wyatt, had a heart attack and died. She was thirty at the time. The responsibility of caring for my siblings and me fell to my oldest sister, Dot. Although Dot was not quite twelve at the time, it was quite common in many black homes for the eldest child to assume the responsibility of an absent or dead parent. Our maternal grandparents had already passed away, and so had our paternal grandmother. Daddy's father was still alive living in Roxie, Mississippi, raising his second family.

Dot said our father was very depressed after my mother's death. Having five young children and a baby to take care of, he went off to work for the Army Corps of Engineers, where he accepted a job as a cook on a barge that went up and down the Mississippi River doing maintenance on the levees. She said before he left, he'd sit up nights, talking to the children about his wishes and dreams for them, telling them how he would miss being with them, but he had to do what was needed in order to make a better living. The only way he could provide properly for his family was to go away to work. The railroad and the Army Corps of Engineers offered the best-paying jobs for an uneducated black man back then. Dot's courage in living up to her imposed responsibilities was admirable.

My father, born May 25, 1912, bore the name Shelby Davis Wyatt, though everyone called him "S.D." Daddy was a handsome man, small of frame at about five feet, six inches and weighing 150 pounds. His skin was smooth and very dark, the color of a strong cup of coffee. His face was graced with high cheekbones, thin lips, and a very distinct nose, shaped kind of like that of an American Indian. I look a lot like my father, except for the nose.

Less than a year after my mother died, hoping to take some of the responsibility away from Dot, Daddy married a woman named Louberta Green. About the same height as my father, Louberta was a full-figured woman with a head full of healthy, thick, black hair, cocoa-colored skin, and a gold-capped tooth in the front, top row of her mouth. Her lips were medium-sized, and she had a full nose.

Her age was a mystery. She couldn't read or write, so it's doubtful she knew her true age. Rumor had it that she was about five years older than our father. This was verified by her great-uncle; that is, if he even knew for sure.

Louberta had six of us to deal with. Dot was the oldest, a tall girl with high cheekbones and the most serious of all of us because she'd had to be. My brother Shelby, Jr., was handsome and quiet. Next came Ruth, the sister I would become closest to, and Herman, my lanky, sly older brother who hoisted me protectively on his lap when one of the other siblings fussed at me about one thing or another and always seemed to have the uncanny ability to make us laugh. Louetta, the closest in age to me, was a little on the wild side, the least conventional of all of us.

For the first five years of my life, we lived near the main highway, Highway 61, which connected Minneapolis to New Orleans. Known as the "Road of the Blues" because so many blues singers had their roots along that highway, the thoroughfare was steeped in tradition, but to me it was simply the local road.

Our home was a "shotgun" house with a front porch, followed by a row of rooms, each opening into the next, from front to back. It was so named because, supposedly, a shotgun could be fired through the house while someone was standing on the porch, and the pellets would fly out the back door without touching a wall. My family used cast-off newspaper as wallpaper. We had a big potbelly stove for heat. Our water for drinking, cooking, and washing came from rain barrels. Daddy bent the eave troughs so they could funnel rainwater into the barrels.

To the north of Fayette at Vicksburg on Highway 61 was

one of America's largest patches of kudzu, a noxious, fast-growing weed imported from Japan for erosion control that threatened to overwhelm the local landscape. To the south before Natchez was the thirty-five-foot-high Emerald Mound, a national historic landmark covering eight acres built by the Natchez Indians.

When I was five, we moved up the road about a half mile from the old house. It had gotten too raggedy for us to live in anymore. The landowner, who owned both properties, offered my father a bigger and better white farmhouse, still on Highway 61, with eight huge rooms. Four other black families, living about a quarter of a mile from one another, formed our very small "neighborhood." We congregated on weekends, late Saturday nights, and Sundays after church services to socialize.

Our new house had screen doors, a screened-in wraparound porch, and masses of colorful flowers in full bloom all over the yard. The yard was beautiful, with many pecan and oak trees for shade. I really enjoyed living in that big old house. Before long, I knew every nook and cranny of our home, which wrapped itself around us like a comfortable old blanket. It became a warm and welcoming place to play, not only for me, but for cousins and friends as well.

Jefferson County was one of the many cotton counties that flourished throughout the state of Mississippi. Some families had their own farms to live on, though the majority—like ours—were rented from white landholders and farmed for a percentage of each year's crop profits.

In addition to cotton, our new accommodations provided land for cows, horses, pigs, and an enormous vegetable garden. Life on the farm was fun and truly rewarding, at least for me as a kid. Farming gave a family some independence, not having to purchase all the necessities for survival from a store. Like our old home, the farmhouse didn't have running water or sanitation facilities or enough furniture to fill the spaciousness, but we did have a truck, a tractor, a freezer, and a car, luxuries that only a few black farmers could hope to attain. With the exception of electricity, we didn't miss the absence of modern conveniences like running water or inside toilets.

We had always had an outhouse, but the one with the new farmhouse was the best we'd ever had. Built like a miniature house, it had two seats and a door that actually locked from the inside, and it was much bigger than the one we'd had before. The new outhouse was built on a concrete slab, whereas the previous one had been just thrown together and had a makeshift door that was tied with pieces of rope to remain closed during usage. The new one sat a good distance from the main house, near the barn, and was never smelly like the other one. It had two steps leading to the door and two little windows for ventilation. Looking back, I see that it was very modern for the times.

We were poor, but we didn't consider being poor a hardship. Everyone around us basically lived the same kind of life. I never felt deprived or unhappy about our living conditions. My father used to say, "You can live in a hut and eat shit with a toothpick and still be happy."

I used to take an ear of corn and shuck it, leaving some of the shucks for hair, lay the corncob out to dry, then fashion a doll with the cob as the body and the shucks as hair. I curled the shucks with a nail, fashioning them into a semblance of a hairstyle. My cousin Robert and I would take a used oil can, clean it, wrap it with rags, and use it for a ball. I still have a scar on my nose from when I was struck by a can while playing. Cardboard boxes were excellent for creating miniature houses and stores. We even made a cardboard house big enough for us kids to play in. One bottle of nail polish was such a big deal to the girls. We could entertain ourselves for hours, painting and repainting our nails. I remember making an awful mess of my hands the first time I was allowed to try painting my nails by myself. Our minds were always at work, creating our own fun, using whatever was available to us for entertainment. I lived a clean, wholesome life, untouched and unspoiled, far different from the materialism of today's society.

My father was a good man who worked hard. I never heard him complain; he always gave my siblings and me an abundance of love and nurturing. He was a very proud and diligent man. Our lifestyle was made by his willingness to work and his wisdom about surviving life in the Deep South. The strong and positive relationship I had with my father was undoubtedly crucial to my developing into a well-adjusted adult.

One of my favorite experiences while living on the farm was the excitement of planting seeds in the ground and watching them grow into vegetables that we would later eat and can. Many times, while I was still too young to help, I watched my stepmother and sisters sitting on the porch, shelling peas and butter beans to make soup for canning. We ate vegetables from our garden as they ripened and canned others for the coming winter months. My brothers and sisters did most of the farm labor, running the farm in Daddy's absence.

After moving into the new house, our father brought home our first wringer-type washer and our first electric iron. My sisters weren't allowed to use them; those appliances were for my stepmother's convenience. Louberta had to be in control of everything, and we all knew that from a very young age. Even though Daddy knew Louberta didn't allow my siblings to use the new conveniences, he gave her complete run of the house—and us as well—rarely questioning her, in order to keep the peace. Louberta never drew her own water for washing; she made Ruth and Louetta do it. She did, however, wash her own laundry and hang it out on the line to dry.

Dot and Ruth still did our wash in a big, old tin tub with a washboard to scrub the clothes clean. My sisters drew the wash water from the well and heated it outside in an old, big, black iron pot on an open fire, then dipped the water into a pail and poured it into the tub, mixing it with cold water to do the wash. When the wash was done, they hung the laundry on a clothesline to dry in the fresh air. They ironed the family's clothes by using the old-fashioned, flat irons that were heated by the fire in the fireplace.

I remember sneaking around the laundry hanging on the line as if a ghost was chasing me, playing and running between the clean sheets billowing in the fresh, open air. Joyously I played while listening for the opening and closing of the screen door, my warning that someone would catch me (most likely Louberta) and reprimand me for touching the clean, white fabric. Ah . . . the fresh smell of line-dried sheets. No other smell compared. No fabric softener ever invented can duplicate that wonderful, fresh scent.

Hogs were killed in the summers and salted down for the winters. The meat that wasn't salted was kept on ice in the icebox for everyday meals. Louberta locked that up to keep track of how much was eaten and rationed out portions as she saw fit. The eggs that were gathered from the henhouses were locked up as well in her big, blue iron trunk, with the key kept in her possession at all times.

She hoarded food for large Sunday dinners which she made for the preacher. Many times my sisters and brothers broke into that old trunk to steal food, usually when Louberta was away spending my father's money on herself. It was the only opportunity to fill our bellies, except when Daddy was home.

Growing up I had a little white-haired puppy with black spots. His hair was short, but for the life of me, I don't remember what breed he was—probably a mutt. His name was Spotty because of his color. Sometimes I'd steal meat out of the icebox for Spotty and me when I thought no one else was around. One day as I was stealing meat, I heard Louberta approaching. Oh Lord! Panic set in, and I didn't know what to do because I knew I'd get a whipping if I was caught. Without thinking, I picked up Spotty and jumped in the icebox, closing the door gently while holding on tight to my puppy. As she came closer I heard her yelling my nickname, Tootise, but I was afraid to answer. After a few screams of "Tootise, Tootise, where are you?" my puppy started barking; she found us. She yanked the icebox door open with a vengeance.

Standing there like a drill sergeant, shaking her head, she yelled, "I can't believe this. Get out of that icebox now!"

I knew by the look on her face that I was in for it. I climbed out sheepishly with Spotty still under my arm, knowing what was coming next. Not only did I get a whipping for stealing the meat, but you can imagine her wrath at me for hiding from her and putting the puppy in the icebox with me. After the whipping I was sent outside with nothing to eat for the rest of the day as punishment.

No one I knew could out-dress Louberta; she was considered one of the best-dressed of the colored women in our town, but the same did not apply to us children. The only time I remember getting new clothes was the beginning of each school year, usually one pair of shoes, one dress dark in color so that it could be worn over and over again, a pair of socks, and a pair of underpants. The boys got a pair of pants, a shirt, and a set of underwear each. Those few articles of clothing had to last us throughout the whole school year. As my brothers got older, they were able to do odd jobs on the weekend to make extra money, which enabled them to buy more for themselves and later helped buy for all of us as well.

It was a long time before I realized that our stepmother had a boyfriend. His name was Mr. Rob Orbinson, but we called him Mr. Rob. As a child, I didn't comprehend what was going on because he was considered a family friend. He frequently came to our house, both day and night. I was led to believe he came by to check up on us in our father's absence. As I grew older, however, I realized that he was Louberta's lover, and I grew to despise both of them.

Daddy either loved Louberta very much or needed her very much, because I told him numerous times about the visits and the goodies—a few peppermint balls or peppermint sticks or Tootsie Rolls—I received from her boyfriend. I don't ever recall a confrontation occurring between the two of them about the boyfriend's visits.

Over the years, I've repeatedly asked myself why our father allowed Louberta's abusive and devious ways to continue. It seemed like an unwritten agreement prevailed: you take care of the house and kids, and I'll take care of you. Children weren't forward in their questioning back in the 1950s; we did pretty much as we were told, or we paid the consequences, and Louberta's consequences were severe. Authority figures *always* had the upper hand, no matter if it was right or wrong.

Louberta aside, life on the farm was good. My favorite chores were helping my brothers milk the cows, gather the eggs, and feed the chickens and other farm animals. I especially loved riding on the tractor, which I learned how to drive at the age of nine.

My family was almost completely self-sufficient when it came to providing food. Seasonings and flour were the only commodities that were purchased from the grocery store. We grew every vegetable that could be grown in the Deep South: potatoes, peas, carrots, okra, mustards, collards and turnip greens, beets, and corn. We even had fish to eat occasionally. My brother Herman loved to fish at a nearby pond. We all knew when he'd been successful, because he'd come down the road with his catch and pole in his hand, usually with his cap turned backwards on his head, and he would be whistling or singing some gospel song loud and clear. His voice always sounded so good to me, but I don't know whether that was because he was a good singer or because I was excited that he'd caught some fish.

The corn was harvested and taken to the mill for grinding into yellow cornmeal. Those trips to the mill represented my biggest chunk of private time with my daddy. It was my opportunity to tell him about all the things that happened during his absence. After I'd finished telling him about what I thought was important, he'd tell me about his job and the people he worked with, and I listened intently to his every word. When we ran out of topics to discuss, I played the game of trying to count the passing cars as we drove to the mill, sometimes falling asleep from the warm sun coming through the windshield.

I loved those times when I was alone with my father; I felt truly special. I loved being with him so much that when he'd announce he was going somewhere, I'd immediately go and hide in the back of the car, lying on the floor, until it was time for him to leave. I waited until we left home before popping up and announcing my presence, knowing we would be too far away for him to turn around and take me back. Of course, I learned much later that he always knew I was back there and was simply humoring me.

My life growing up during the early years was like living in a big backyard. We left that backyard occasionally when we had a reason—school, church, a trip to the mill—but even on these excursions, we stayed within the black community. Aside from those trips, most of my awareness of life occurred in that backyard, with my siblings and occasionally with cousins, as oblivious to the rest of Fayette as I was to the rest of the world. Things that happened outside of that yard had nothing to do with me, at least in the beginning.

My awareness of the white community and the unspoken rules between blacks and whites came gradually. Louberta took a job as a domestic, working for the Melton family at their estate called the Melton Plantation, and one day I went with my father to pick her up after work. Their house sat about a quarter of a mile off the main road and was the biggest and most beautiful one I'd ever seen. As we drove up the road that led to the front entrance of the house, I was thrilled by the sights of the oak, pecan, and magnolia trees draped in Spanish moss that lined the road. Louberta wasn't quite ready when we arrived. Daddy sent me in through the kitchen entrance to let her know that we would be waiting outside when she finished.

As I entered, a little white girl with long, blonde curls came bounding in to tell Louberta goodbye. She was about my age, nine or so. She befriended me so I started to play with her. After Louberta finished up the cleaning, she turned to say goodbye to the girl, "Good-bye, Miz Susan," she said. "See you tomorrow."

Miz? I was shocked to hear her addressing a child my age as she would an adult. In front of the girl, I asked, "Why are you calling her 'Miz Susan'?" Without warning, Louberta gave me a backhand smack across the mouth and told me to shut up and go to the car, never offering any kind of explanation. Needless to say, I felt dumbfounded and ashamed to be slapped in front of Susan. I made my way to the car totally confused and sat quietly in the backseat without mentioning the incident to my father. When Louberta got in the car, she didn't mention it either. She started talking to my father as if nothing had happened.

That incident stuck with me.

A short time later, Louberta, Louetta, and I were in the town's only department store, buying our usual before-school-opens clothes on credit. Blacks were denied the privilege of trying anything on; the size had to be guessed. After Louberta finished her purchases, the owner turned to her and asked, "Is that all, Auntie?"

Again, I turned around dumbfounded. I remembered the incident with the little girl, but I couldn't stop myself. I popped the question again, "Mama, why did that man call you 'Auntie'?" She must have been very embarrassed, because she just looked at me and hissed under her breath for me to shut up. I was totally confused because I knew Louberta couldn't possibly be his aunt, so why would he call her that?

It was only when these experiences began building up that I sought an explanation from my father. He said calling the older generation of blacks *aunt* and *uncle* was the white man's way of showing "false respect." As a child, I had thought the expressions on the faces of the black people when they were addressed that way reflected appreciation, but now I knew their expressions conveyed barely disguised disgust. They always said the usual, "*Thank you, Suh*," or, "*Yessir, that's all for this time.*"

My father told me that blacks had to call all white people, even those younger than they were, *Mister, Miz,* or *Sir.* Blacks, on the other hand, were only known by their first names, or such titles as *aunt* or *uncle.* From that conversation, I finally understood why Louberta addressed that little white girl the way she had.

My father went on to tell me if a white person considered a black person too outspoken, that person was called names, such as *uppity, trouble-maker,* or *a nigger that needed to be watched.* This was after the days when there were beatings or hangings for insurrection against the white man's rules, but he said white people found other ways to deal with blacks who stood up for themselves. One method was cutting off a black family's credit or immediately forcing the repayment of old debts.

My father told me many stories about how things were when he was a young boy growing up. He said Fayette had been very different in years past. When he went into town with his parents to get the supplies they needed for the week, he rode on the back of their wagon, which was pulled by two mules. The buildings then along Main Street were older and shabbier, and on Saturdays, blacks spilled aimlessly out from the sidewalks and filling stations into the street, being careful not to bump into a white person.

He not only had to understand the rules, but he had to know the social behavior of a young black boy in a white community. No matter the age of a black man, in the eyes of a white man, he was still a *boy.* If a white person was walking down the sidewalk, a black person had to step aside until the white person passed. White people always had the right of way. If a white man stopped a black adult for conversation, he or she had to lower his eyes to the ground so as not to look the white man in the eye. Most of the conversations were one-sided, with the black person nodding and agreeing with whatever the white person was saying.

The story he told me about blacks wearing white shirts stuck with me the most. He said that when he was a young man, they had to wear work shirts Monday through Saturday. White shirts were only allowed on Sundays. If blacks were caught wearing one on any other day, there had to be a good explanation for it. A funeral was one of the few exceptions.

My father was not a book-educated man; he was rather simple and straightforward, projecting only one face to the public, that of a strong-willed black man doing what he had to do to survive in the white man's world. I don't remember how my father related to whites when I was young, whether he followed the protocol of lowering his eyes and being deferential, because whites were not a daily part of my life. We were taught to stay as far away from them as possible. Years later, I learned that the isolation was instituted by my father for our own protection; Daddy knew all too well how white men treated black women and girls.

Our lives consisted, mainly, of going to school, going to church, and staying home doing chores. The black community turned to God when there seemed to be no other place to seek solace; our folks relied heavily on the power of prayers. The older blacks I knew were wise, caring, courageous, honest, and full of love, and we children trusted and believed in them. They were like an extension of our own immediate family.

As was the custom then, churches were named after the family who donated the land on which they were built, and ours was named Taylor's Chapel Baptist Church after the Taylor family. Since no single church in the area could afford a full-time minister, we shared the minister's time; thus, our church only hosted on the first Sunday of each month.

Church day was a day to dress in our Sunday best. No matter how poor a family was, everyone had a special outfit to wear to church. Sometimes, attending church was more like going to a fashion show than to a church service. The women all wore large hats, gloves, and multicolored clothing. That was the only time I remember seeing so many women so well dressed, wearing makeup and Red Fox stockings, which were, as the name suggests, bright red and matched the color of their lipstick.

My only dressy dress I vividly remember was a white, sheer dress with big white roses embroidered throughout. It came with two ribbon belts attached at each side of the waist, which were tied in a bow at the back. Tiny, white buttons closed the upper back, and a "can-can," a stiffly starched undergarment, was sewn in around the waist, which made it stick out, away from my legs. I still have that dress, old and fragile as it is.

The church building played many roles within the black community, serving as a place for social events and important meetings, as well as for worship. My family arrived early every first Sunday; the early birds had a chance to talk and catch up on what was happening in the community, for many families didn't have a chance to see each other except for on that first Sunday. They exchanged news, information, and recipes of new foods that they had learned how to cook in the white homes.

Outside on that church lawn, before services began, was when I first heard tidbits of information about integration. I was around ten, old enough to know something important was being said but young enough to not have the older folks worry about my listening in. The grown-ups always left the children in a small group close by so they could keep an eye on us, but far enough away, so they thought, for them to talk privately. The men were usually huddled in one group, the women in another, exchanging conversations they'd heard during the week.

I was and still am a pretty inconspicuous person but while I played around, I listened intently. Most of the talk was coming from women who worked as domestics in white homes.

"They's worried about a revolution comin'," Ella Mae whispered to Louberta one Sunday.

"Yes, they is," someone else said. "Listen to Ella Mae, using such big word!"

Ella Mae continued as if she hadn't heard. "I overheard Miz Katherine telling Miz Lizziebeth that this Civil Rights Movement was comin' here so's us black folk would have the same rights as them. Now, can you believe that?"

Louberta rolled her eyes. "Well, you know that's never gonna happen."

"Yeah," Ella Mae sighed. "But now wouldn't it be somethin' if it did?"

Those conversations were whispered in such low tones that it made me wonder if the people were speaking of something evil. The best place for overhearing those conversations was outside church where that seemed to have been our community's gathering place.

Going to church was expected; sickness was the only acceptable reason to miss. Sunday school was held before the regular service, which started at 11:00 a.m. and lasted until 2:00 p.m., unless a special service was scheduled. A rally was considered a special service, which was also a way to raise funds for the church and in that case the service lasted much longer.

The children often squirmed throughout the long services, but their behavior was generally ignored. During the summers, when the sweltering temperatures inside the church rose accordingly, fans were passed around as cheap air conditioning. Every adult was offered a fan, but hardly any of us kids received one. The fans advertised funeral homes, or some type of burial insurance company, and sometimes political announcements. Even if a kid did manage to find a fan and hold onto it, an usher would come along and take it away to give to a grown-up who didn't have one. In order to keep my fan, I hid it when I saw the usher coming. I slipped it behind me, resting my back against it until the usher passed, easing it out only when I thought it was safe. To have a fan of your own was a big deal for kids.

My favorite fan was the one with the face of Jesus Christ on it. I often stared at that face with its deep-set blue eyes which seemed to be staring back at me. Sometimes, I found myself talking to the face on the fan as if it would speak back to me. I told Jesus about my hurtful stepmother and how I sometimes wished she were dead. I could share all of my childhood secrets with that face, things I couldn't share with anyone else, even though the face of Jesus was white.

Nothing is quite like the sights and sounds of a rural, black, Baptist church. The services began with a song from one of the deacons, and then he led us into prayer, which always ended with a short version of what the content of the sermon would be about when the preacher took over the pulpit. The ending of the sermon was always the same: the warning: "Satan is busy!" This was the preacher's way of informing the congregation that we had to keep living our lives by the Bible teachings during the week, not just on Sundays. The first time I heard those words, fear was instilled in me.

The congregation of our Southern Baptist Church was lively; people shouting, screaming, and stomping their feet, a real whoop-and-holler kind of service. The minister stood for the delivery of his sermon, bellowing his beginning words like the angry sounds of the mighty Mississippi when a storm was blowing in, then slowly diminishing the roar to the rumble of a stream, and then to the likeness of a trickling brook. The congregation followed suit, the crescendos of their moaning and groaning increasing and diminishing, in accordance with the minister's delivery.

During the sermon, one of the mothers of our church, Mrs. Ella Scott, would start jumping up and down, tears running down her face, overcome by the sheer power of the minister's words. After she composed herself, she never failed to start singing "The Lord Is My Shepherd," while her tears fell freely. The more emotional the congregation became, the more successful the sermon was judged to be.

I love and have always loved Baptist singing, the kind of spiritual revival songs that reach way down deep into the soul. When the choir sang, they conveyed the songs to our souls and let them warmly seep through our bones. All the church windows were open during the hot, muggy months, and anyone driving by could hear the singing and shouting.

Once the service was under way, fans waved in the air, feet tapped, people moaned and groaned, and a multitude of *Amen*s echoed throughout the congregation. Most of the time, the bobbing hats atop the women's heads and the waving fans prevented us little people from seeing very much.

One time a woman in the pew in front of me started to shout. She jumped up, hollering, "Lawd, have *mussee!*" Then she threw her hat and her purse up in the air, waving and throwing her arms everywhere. With the billowing sleeves of her dress, her arms looked like outstretched wings, as if she might take off and fly into the air. The spirit must have welled up and overtaken her, for she threw her hands behind her and smacked me squarely in the face. Not knowing why she hit me, I retaliated by hitting her back. She wasn't even aware of what I had done with all the commotion going on. The ushers had a hard time trying to contain that woman. It always amazed me that after such an emotional gesture, the women sat back down and composed themselves as if nothing had happened.

Most churches in the area had two rallies a year, the anniversary date of the church's completion and the pastor's anniversary, the date he became the minister of that particular church. Rallies gave the women a chance to show off their cooking skills with fried chicken, corn bread stuffing, potato salad, baked glazed hams, macaroni and cheese casseroles, sweet potato pies, and an assortment of pound cakes. Two or three days were needed to do all the shopping, cutting, chopping, and baking.

I used to love those times at our house because they reminded me of Christmas. The kitchen smelled so good from the cooking aromas of the different foods, and, along with my sisters and brothers, we were permitted to taste the baking. My stepmother made a little sample of the pound cake to try out before the final one was baked to make sure it tasted perfect. My favorite thing to do was to sit on the floor by the big, old, wood-burning stove, sopping up the cake bowl with my finger after the batter was poured into a pan and put into the oven. I remember sitting there, watching the wood burn in the stove, as if by my watching, the sample would get done faster. As I waited, I'd imagine the taste of the cake on my lips.

When the special service for the rally concluded, the food baskets were laid out for the congregation. As a courtesy to all the women, the pastor had to sample the food from every basket, and what he couldn't eat, he had to take home. By doing so, he wouldn't appear to favor one woman's cooking over another, which would have caused great offense.

Everyone tasted everyone else's food, even though they all brought the same basic menu. Quickly, it became known which baskets held the best fried chicken, the best stuffing, the best cakes and pies, and who made them. Those baskets were targeted first. Easily, a family could go home with as much food as they had brought, and it wouldn't necessarily be their own food.

If someone noticed that a member of a family did not attend church, a plate was prepared and sent home for the absent person. With all the food, singing, and speeches that went into the making of a good rally, oftentimes strangers who were just passing by stopped, were fed, and were sent on their way with an extra plate of food.

The men didn't do any of the cooking or baking; they made donations, which was another way to help raise funds for the church. Other churches were invited to participate, because rallies were also intended to help raise money for a church's maintenance, remodeling, and repairs and to purchase new pews, pianos, and other church necessities. At the end of each rally, the secretary stood and read the minutes, informing the congregation how much money was raised, and then shared other news concerning the church. Those were the best memories of my childhood.

2
The Awakening of Fayette

The women were all gathered around Miz Beulah in the yard outside church. "I was in the kitchen cooking and doing chores the other day," she whispered, "when Miz Kate was on the phone talking and didn't think I was listening."

"Mm, hmm," someone said as the others drew closer.

"Miz Kate was saying, 'This movement is trying to give niggers equal rights, the same as us; now, isn't that something? They expect us to pay 'em more money!'"

Eyes rolled.

Miz Beulah lowered her voice. "When I heard that, I stuck close to her so's I could hear everything she was saying. Figured it had to be somethin' important to have her all worked up. I'm standin' there moppin' the kitchen floor when suddenly I hear her say, 'Well, you know Beulah doesn't have a television, so she won't be a problem. She won't know what's going on.'"

"Talkin' like you wasn't in the room!" gasped one of the women.

"Right. Chile, I really felt like wringin' her neck just like I was squeezin' the water out of that mop."

"Beulah!"

"Well, Miz Kate ain't an easy woman to work for."

"Amen to that," someone shouted.

"Do you think she's right?" Beulah asked, her eyes roaming from woman to woman. "About this movement?"

Some shrugged, some sighed; most looked away.

Figure 2. Martha's senior portrait

Miz Kate was right in a way. Most of the elders in the black community of Fayette couldn't read or write, and the majority of families, like ours, didn't have a television. I knew very few who even had radios. We thus relied heavily on each other for sources of information, and the Beulahs in our midst were important news sources. Ironically, it was the white community that was informing us—albeit indirectly—about integration.

The black women who worked for prominent white families as maids or cooks were overhearing conversations about "this movement" from their white employers, and their employers' friends when they came to visit. These black women knew how to be inconspicuous, working diligently, while taking in as much of the conversations as they could at the same time. Blacks were very adept at appearing to be a bit short in the mental capacities. They knew that's how the whites viewed them. The advantage was that these maids and cooks heard virtually everything their employers and anyone else around them said. Their employers treated them as insignificant beings, never paying attention or being careful about what they said. And, oh, did the black women I knew have good memories! They could repeat those conversations verbatim.

The men went into town and mingled on the streets on Friday evenings and Saturdays to "pick up" the rumblings of the white people. However, if there was any gossip going around town and someone wanted to know the whole story, the thing to do was just ask those black maids. They could tell stories much better than the men and give more in-depth details. It wasn't called gossiping back then; it was called "news." Each maid had a different story to tell, and she'd pass the stories on to her husband and to other maids of the community. They all exchanged stories. They didn't necessarily know what some of the words they overheard meant, or they might mispronounce a word here and there, but among themselves, they somehow figured out the meaning of those unfamiliar words.

Mostly, it seemed, the white women who employed maids or cooks were worried that this new freedom for blacks would cause them to have to pay higher wages, with their employees possibly working shorter hours. They also wondered how long they would continue to work for them if they refused to pay more.

The white community had major concerns, but so did the black community. The black community's concerns were just very different. They mostly wondered, "Why in the world would anyone want to help us colored folks?" And they worried about what the consequences might be if people *did* try to help us colored folks. Gathered on the church's front lawn before Sunday services began, people relayed the latest "news" to one another, with concern on their faces and panic in their voices.

"Vest," I heard my father say to his friend Sylvester Tillman, "what are we going to do?"

In response Sylvester sighed, "Pee, I just don't know. Guess we'll have to wait and see what the white folks do." Mr. Vest, as we called him, always called my dad "Pee." I never heard him call him anything else but that.

Even though Supreme Court decisions and new laws were attacking the Jim Crow ways of separate but equal education, employment, and the use of public facilities, the black adults around me in Fayette, Mississippi, remained totally unaffected by such goings-on, and mixed in their opinions. Some were excited, but many were fearful about the changes the movement was going to bring and the potential repercussions of those changes. "Equality" was a foreign concept. People my family knew and associated with were afraid that a disruption of this magnitude would cause more harm than good. Women who were used to taking in washing and/or ironing at their homes, those working as maids/cooks, or picking up pecans to sell, or maintaining other odd jobs, worried their income sources might dry up after the movement changed things. The black community had accepted its place in society, simply because it had never known things any other way, and wasn't quite prepared for the changes that the movement was going to bring about. The unfairness of the system had always been evident, but it was only spoken about behind closed doors, and even then, it was usually after the children had gone to bed.

This news of "the movement" caused a wave of paranoia in our tiny community. Blacks and whites became very distrustful of each other. All conversations concerning racial issues were whispered as if walls could talk. Blacks even became suspicious of one another. Maids whispered to each other, afraid of being overheard by someone other than a maid. They feared for their jobs and couldn't take the risk of their employers hearing about their passing on information.

Black parents became tense and irritable, on edge. We children sensed that during times of such emotional distress it was better to stay out of the way and not disturb them. I was far better off staying to myself, merely observing the grown-ups, keeping my mouth shut, while my ears were wide open, taking in as much as possible before being sent outside to play.

Black farmers like my father worried about their farms and their credit being taken away. Most didn't own the land they farmed, but rather sharecropped with a white landowner. Now, my father wondered, would the landowner ask us to move? Would he still be able to farm the land for a percentage of the profits? Would our lives go on as before? These questions made for a very uneasy existence.

While eavesdropping in our home, I'd hear bits and pieces of conversations between my father and some of the neighbors. Mostly, they wondered about receiving advances, as they had in the past, to buy whatever supplies or seeds they needed to plant their crops. If they required a loan, would the white bank owners give them the loan? My father's biggest worry was, "Will the bank call in my loan on the tractor?" He had purchased it on credit. Credit carried our family and many other families through the winter months, and debts were settled with money received from the profits of harvested crops.

All of these unknown factors about sharecropping for a white landowner prompted our father to make the decision to move out of the big farmhouse, where we had lived for six years. We moved to Poplar Hill, an area about five miles out-side of town, into a house owned by a black landowner, Mr. Bole Riley. This house was much smaller than the previous one, but we made do with what we had. Once Daddy made up his mind about the move, he gave up his job with the corp of engineers and turned to full-fledged farming. Louberta still worked for the Melton family. She didn't help Daddy with the farming; that job remained up to my siblings.

Our new home became even more cramped because shortly after we moved in, Louberta moved her great-aunt and -uncle, Oz and Julia Tillman, in to live with us. They were growing too old to take care of themselves, so our five-room house became packed, sardine-style. Louberta put an-other bed in the bedroom Louetta and I shared, and her aunt and uncle became our roommates. The tight arrangement was suffocating, but we couldn't say or do anything about it; Louberta did as Louberta pleased. Louetta and I both re-sented the intrusion and wondered why she didn't put them in *her* room if she wanted them there so badly. We had many talks about that arrangement but kept it to ourselves.

We had to endure the snores and farts and all the other idiosyncrasies that go along with being old, which made us ashamed to have any of our friends over. The aunt's mind was failing, and the only thing she seemed to remember was the nineteenth of the month when they received their Social Security check. She constantly smelled of urine. She had no teeth but continually wanted to eat apples from the tree in our backyard. My job was to fetch them for her, and oh, how I loathed that imposition. The apples had to be cut in half so she could scrape the fruit out of the peel, spoonful by spoon-ful.

I used to play tricks on her because I knew how forgetful she was. I'd hear her calling, "Tootise, Tootise, come here, gal." If I took too long she'd call again, this time in a more irritated voice, "Gal, you hear me calling you; come here this minute." I'd finally go see what she wanted. Never a "please" or "thank you."

I think I hated that woman for invading my space, what little I had, and I hated my stepmother even more for bringing her there to live. Louberta and my father had a few spats about the arrangement, but in the end she won. The only time I remember Mrs. Julia saying anything was to ask for something to eat. She never wore underpants, which made me even more hateful of her and her ways. I'm not sure if she simply forgot to put any on, or if she didn't care at that point in her life; either way she was such a burden.

The uncle, "Mr. Tillman" as we called him, kept us entertained with stories about his upbringing. My favorite story was the one he would tell us about his father being a slave. He was a very wise old man. Even though his wife hardly ever remembered who he was, he remained patient and loving toward her, always attending to her needs. I don't know how he did it. I never witnessed him losing his temper or his patience with her. It was impossible for him to have any kind of conversation with her anymore, so he'd spend his day talking and telling us stories until we got restless and went outside to play. Once outside, we usually stayed until dusk or until we got called in.

I was fourteen years old on April 3, 1964, when tragedy struck my family. My much adored nineteen-year-old brother, Herman, was shot and killed. Many conflicting stories surrounded his death, but the general consensus was that he was shot by mistake—because from a distance he looked like the intended victim. The man who murdered him was hiding under a parked car when he fired six bullets into Herman's body. Herman was rushed to the hospital, where he died five days later. The days Herman was in the hospital were very intense, as my family struggled with the biggest tragedy we had ever experienced. Then there were the preparations for his burial. Our house was packed each night, up until the service, with family, friends and well-wishers bringing pots and containers of food. There was hardly ever a private moment to grieve.

The following Sunday, while standing in the yard waiting to leave for the funeral, I saw my father take a drink for the first time. He took a bottle of liquor out of his coat pocket, tipped it to his lips, and then passed it along to my oldest brother, S. D., Jr., to do the same. It was also the first time I saw my daddy cry, which made me feel very sad for him among all the other feelings and emotions I was dealing with myself.

En route to the funeral, I sat staring out the car window, seeing and hearing nothing but the heavy rain pouring down. The older generation used to say that when it rained that hard on the day of a funeral, the dead person's soul would surely be washed away to heaven. I hoped that was true because then my brother's soul was on its way to heaven.

Not until I was sitting in the church did the true reality of Herman's death hit me. I sat staring at the stone-cold casket, knowing I would never see my brother again or hear his laughter or his voice. Memories flashed through my mind of how witty and funny he was, how he loved to retell stories and jokes he'd heard from the older folks, but at the same time, he retold them in a way that made my siblings and me laugh. I'd laugh so hard until tears would roll down my face while I held my aching sides. Closing my eyes, I pictured him grinning from ear to ear, bringing home a string of fish. Now I would never be able to touch him again or feel him hug me or hear his voice singing as he made his way home. At that moment, the bottom fell out of my world, and I sobbed so loudly I almost drowned out the music coming from the organ.

My family knew who the murderer was, but little was done in the name of justice; it was simply viewed as another black-on-black crime. The murderer spent six months in jail, pending trial, but after the trial was over, he was a free man. My family was never given a real explanation of why my brother was killed, but we had to live in the same town with Herman's murderer, watching him go about his life, while we struggled to get on with ours. My oldest brother, S. D., Jr., was so upset that he moved to Chicago a few months after Herman's death, where he still lives. He said he couldn't live in Fayette anymore and watch the man who had killed his brother walk around as if he hadn't done a thing. We all understood his feelings, and my father gave him his blessings.

S. D., Jr., was one of many to venture north at the time, although his reason for leaving differed from the others who moved in search of greater opportunity. Word throughout the South was that above the Mason-Dixon Line lay an abundance of riches—good jobs, social equality, and cultural diversity, the kind of newly unearthed treasures that had yet to pan out for most blacks in Dixie, one hundred years after emancipation.

I can remember a few families, mainly distant neighbors, that moved from Fayette. The Bias family, the Allens, and the Scott family moved to Chicago. Some of the Anderson family moved to Los Angeles. The Thompson family moved to Harlem, and some of the Tillmans moved to Detroit. I heard about other families that moved as time passed, but I wasn't directly associated with them. Those who left didn't all move at the same time; it was a gradual progression, sometimes after the Ku Klux Klan burned a cross in a yard. Usually, the older children left, sometimes taking younger siblings with them, leaving the parents behind with promises of coming back to get them when they were established in different cities.

Occasionally, a child might return for the parents, but more often than not, the parents remained on their homesteads, clinging to hopes of better lives for their children in larger cities. Southern blacks thought any black who had the good fortune to achieve even a simple education in the North was going to be, just by virtue of this fact, better off than a black in the South.

The move north that affected me most was when John Mayer, a boy I'd grown up with and I loved with all my young heart, left school at age sixteen and moved to Chicago. I'd been certain that John was the boy I'd eventually grow up to marry some day. We shared the same birthday, month, date, and year, and his family and mine had celebrated our birthdays together each year. I felt completely lost without John around. We stayed in contact with each other for a while, but it was never the same. I truly missed my childhood friend and my playmate.

My father brought home our first television set in 1965. By that time I had entered my first year of high school, and all of my siblings had left home, having either married or gone off to live on their own. Even after we had television, I wasn't aware of much that happened outside of Fayette. Television to me, a typical teenager, was "Lassie," "The Rifleman," and "Popeye." I wasn't interested in the news.

A group of our most prominent black citizens of Jefferson County got together and organized mass meetings to be held every Thursday night at 8:00 p.m. to prepare the community for the movement and the changes it was going to bring to Fayette. Most of the people who spoke at these meetings were the preachers, the school principal, and those who were respected and looked up to by the black community. The location changed to a different church each week. This was due partly to throw off any unwanted presence or interference, especially from the KKK. Some people walked to these meetings, not wanting their cars to be seen, yet the parking lot was always filled to the brim from the people who lived outside of the area. Churches were packed, with people spilling out onto the steps and lawn. If you wanted to hear what was being said, you had to go early. Late arrivals had to strain their ears, while standing outside near the door or near the windows, trying their best to gather what they could from the speeches that were being made inside. Sometimes those meetings didn't break up until late into the night.

While I was aware of what was going on, I was not at all involved in the cause. Children were not permitted inside the churches; only those of voting age and older gained entrance. But, sometimes for adventure, Mr. Vest's son, Man (pronounced Mane), would drive his twin siblings, Rose, and brother, Ed, and Louetta and me by the hosting church to see what we could see and hear what we could hear. One night when we went I saw the car of my brother's killer parked on the church grounds. Without giving it a second thought, I picked up a huge rock, threw it at the car, and broke the windshield. When I told the others what I had done, we all high-tailed it back to the truck and Man didn't waste any time taking off.

At sixteen I must admit I was more concerned with love than civil rights. Trying to fill the void in my heart left by John, I noticed a boy in my class with a handsome, strong face, a neatly trimmed crew cut, and a body built for football. He was not very tall, about five feet, five inches, but his height wasn't really that important, because he seemed to have everything else I thought I wanted: courage, openness, and good looks. Most of all, he drove his own car, a 1956 black-and-white Chevy, and he seemed experienced. By that, I mean he was daring; he smoked and joked around, as if he didn't have a care in the world. He played baseball and football and was outgoing—everything I wasn't. Some high school kids considered him to be a little on the wild side, compared to my sheltered upbringing.

His name was Lee. (For my children's sake, I'm using the boy's middle name only.) Being too shy to speak to him, I went home each day after school and tried to think of ways to get him to notice me. I dreamed up all sorts of clever schemes to capture his attention; however, in the light of day, my ideas seemed silly and childish.

On the first day of our junior year, Mr. Berry, the principal, called an assembly for the student body but especially for the juniors and seniors. He was delivering a welcome-back speech. He also wanted to inform us of big changes that would be taking place at the beginning of that school year. I had been five years old in 1954 when the Supreme Court ruled on the *Brown vs. Board of Education* case, declaring racial segregation in public schools to be unconstitutional. For twelve years, Jefferson County had simply ignored Supreme Court decisions concerning the rules of integration. And now, Mr. Berry was about to tell us, the time had finally come for those rules to be put into place. At the beginning of the 1966 school year, four black students in their junior year at Liddell High School—Brenda Stone, Alice Coleman, Ed Dunlap, and Charles Harris—had been selected to be sent to the white school, Jefferson High, to break the color barrier: it was going to be the first year of integration for our town.

It says something about my state of mind that the announcement that day paled in my memory in comparison to the prank that Lee pulled off. During the program, suddenly a tiny little garter snake (a small snake usually seen in gardens to help keep pests away) began slithering through the crowd. Lee had kept that snake in his pocket so as not to draw attention to himself beforehand. When it was noticed, everyone sitting close to Lee started scrambling to get away. That commotion didn't go over very well with the principal and the faculty, but Lee was never punished for his actions because no one besides me knew who had brought the snake in. I was awed by how daring the move was. I was smitten. Lee and I began dating.

If I was, at the time, oblivious to what was going on outside my limited world, so were most of those in my community. The debate over black power, the movement among black Americans emphasizing racial pride and social justice that was sweeping the country, stirred up less publicity and anxiety in rural Mississippi than in the North. The towns and cities that were talked about on television seemed to be in a different world from the one I lived in. The simple truth was sit-ins, marches, and protests were remote to me. I couldn't imagine living in a world full of black doctors or lawyers or other professionals working for the movement.

The blacks in our community outnumbered the whites about five to one, making their potential strength very real, indeed. However, although the NAACP had come to our area in the early sixties, knowledge about their activities wasn't widespread. The meetings were held secretly in small churches. How was I to know that what I saw on television would ever have anything to do with Fayette?

On long, lazy, Saturday evenings, after dinner and dishes were done, our family usually migrated outdoors. During those late summer evenings, the neighbors of the community gathered at one house to sit outside on the porch, relaxing. The grown-ups sat together talking and watching the sunset, while the older children sat on the steps, talking amongst themselves.

The smaller children played stickball or hopscotch in the yard, kicking up the dust while the dogs chased after us. Sometimes, we would join hands, form a ring, and sing songs such as "Little Sally Walker," or we'd jump rope to the tune of "Ice cream, soda water, cream on top, tell me the name of your sweetheart," songs that had been passed down from generation to generation.

I enjoyed those special, peaceful times. In the black people's world, I was free and safe. I had no racial problems, and I lived in virgin territory as far as the movement was concerned.

And then everything changed.

When September rolled around and Brenda, Alice, Ed, and Charles were seniors, our educational leaders wanted more black students to attend the white school. I, too, was a senior and was told that I was being considered as an applicant for that year along with my friend Bob. I never considered myself a candidate for integration and had no idea what challenges I would be facing on a day-to-day basis.

When Mr. Berry, the high school principal, asked the teachers to select more students for Jefferson High School, I didn't mind being chosen by one of my favorite teachers and role models, Mrs. Catherine Knox, my English teacher.

Once new students were chosen, the selected group was then called in to meet with Mr. Berry and a few of the high school teachers, who made up the "Integration Committee," as I called them. This committee's purpose was to get us prepared for our new journey. Mr. Berry and the teachers informed us many times during those meetings how significant our actions would be for the cause. They did their best to prepare us. We were informed that the burden of racism was largely placed on blacks, because we were the ones who had to constantly prove ourselves in the eyes of an unjust society. Mr. Berry told us that we had to learn how to take the worst, and we had to understand that violence was never an option.

I thought it was a bit silly to give us such lessons in mental brutality, for we were merely going to a different school. The teachers and principal kept encouraging us to ask questions. "Don't be afraid to tell us what is on your mind!" I truly didn't know enough to know what questions to ask. But as I sat in that cluttered little office, listening and trying to comprehend all that was being said, I felt my confidence diminishing.

"In time," Mr. Berry said "what you are doing will influence the course of American history." That was one of our main objectives, and we were to remember that at all times. We would be watched, not just by the whites, but by the blacks as well. We were told to keep our heads up and to ignore the racial slurs that we, undoubtedly, would hear. We had to be strong and hold onto the real reasons we were being sent there: to fight for equal education and equal opportunities for all people.

My only experience around white people was those once-a-year school shopping trips or the few times I'd gone with my father to the mill or to pick up Louberta from work. Truthfully, I had more interaction with the trees along the road than I did with the white population. Our worlds were so far apart that I had no real opinion as to what it would be like to interact with them on a daily basis.

Parents were required to give their permission before any student could be considered, and looking back, I'm really surprised my father allowed me to attend the white school. Daddy never asked me if that was something I wanted to do or not; as a matter of fact, we never discussed it together at all. He must have felt I was strong enough to handle it because after meeting with the Integration Committee, he gave his consent.

"You've always been a talker," my father told me before sending me off on that first morning of school integration. "You're gonna have to talk less and listen more. The less said, the better."

I nodded.

"Never trust a white person," he instructed. "And don't worry about what they think of you. White people see all black people as the same. It's not important how they see you; it's important how you see yourself."

I nodded.

"You're gonna be afraid, but you can't show fear or weakness. Be on guard, though—these people are not going to be your friends—and think before acting. Don't do anything that will make you look stupid in their eyes."

I began picturing every white person at that school as my foe, ready to stab me in the back at a moment's notice.

"Tootise, if you find money lying around anywhere, leave it. Don't pick it up."

That was strange. I'd never found any money before, so I asked, "Why, Daddy?"

"White folks think all colored people steal, and they have a habit of leaving money lying around just to see if it suddenly goes missing when a colored person's around. It's a test. Don't fall prey to it. No matter what you see or where you see it, leave it there. No exceptions."

"Yes, Daddy." I never liked confrontations, and he seemed to be telling me that a giant one was coming on. By the time our talk was over I felt as though a heavy blanket had been placed on top of me, one that I couldn't wait to get out from under.

There were only ten of us, including the four students from the previous year, that first morning when we boarded the bus to be driven to the white school. We looked like little soldiers going off to fight a war, only we were unarmed except for our own internal weapons: integrity, beliefs, and self-esteem. We sat huddled together on the bus, talking. Once there, we fell silent. When the bus driver opened the door, I felt paralyzed with fear. As we stood to make a single line, the principal of our new school, Mr. Robert Gavin, and a handful of teachers gathered out front to greet us, and the white students made a corridor through which we had to pass. Never before had I seen so many white faces in one place at one time, in my entire life. And they were all staring at us.

My legs, as I stood, were trembling so badly, I wasn't sure I was going to make it without stumbling. Walking from the bus to the front doors of the school seemed like miles rather than a few feet, but I kept my head high looking straight ahead, trying not to make eye contact with anyone. The white kids did not taunt or jeer at us that first day. They were very quiet and just stared, their eyes following us into the school and our classrooms. I think they must have been warned, because no one threw anything. No one hollered out loud that day. That would come later.

When I returned home that first night, my father was full of questions. "How were you treated? Were you scared?" I answered yes to the second question, but the first question left me pondering. Then he wanted to know how the teachers had treated me. For that, I had no straight answer, because everything about that day was very unsettling. The teachers spent more time in the hallway talking with each other than talking to the students. After talking with my father and answering his questions to the best of my ability, I was left alone with the thoughts jumping around in my brain. Exhausted, I finally fell asleep, but not before realizing I was going to have to face the same situation the very next day and many days to come.

As new and unfamiliar as this world was to me, it had to be just as new and unfamiliar to the white students as well. Going to school with blacks sure wasn't the same for them as having blacks working as maids in their homes, or doing field work for their fathers. They had not been raised to believe this was any possible version of America.

Our very existence at their school constituted a powerful change, but at the time I could not grasp what that change constituted or why it was so all-mighty important for me to attend an all-white school. I felt as though I was in a foreign universe, unknowledgeable about the customs of the white race or how to relate to them. As for rights, I didn't know what rights were. Growing up, I didn't recall ever being angry that I had to drink out of a different fountain than whites, or thinking that having to go to a different restroom was a violation of my rights, or that going to a segregated school was anything other than just plain going to school. I frankly didn't care at that age whether or not I could go into a restaurant frequented by whites, sit down, and order a meal. I had no reason to think about it or even want to; our family had never gone to a restaurant to eat anyway. Having grown up in such a depressed area and having never experienced life in any other part of the country I had simply accepted the status quo.

The hollering and taunts and hisses of "nigger" began on day two, and I could do little more than recoil from the looks of hatred and the racial slurs directed at me. During the school hours, I felt so far away from my own school, my teachers, my friends, and my family. Keeping the "no violence" rule in mind, the question that haunted me the most was, what would I do if someone physically tried to hurt me? I felt like running away and leaving it all behind. I wanted to run back to the safety and shelter of my teachers and friends at Liddell High, back to the safety and love of my father, my siblings, and my neighbors. The thoughts that continuously pounded through my mind were, "Why do I have to be here?" and "Why did I have to be thrown into such an unfriendly world of obvious hatred and disgust?" Never in my life had I experienced such blatant, soul-draining hostility.

While standing outside on the school grounds one day just having a quiet moment to myself, I saw a shiny object lying in the grass. As I approached it, I saw that it was money, a quarter. Instead of immediately reaching down and picking it up, I stood with my foot on it, looking around inconspicuously to see if anyone else had seen it and wondering if anyone was watching me to see if I'd pick it up. The conversation I'd had with my father that first morning kept going through my mind. When I was satisfied that no one had seen the quarter, I bent down and scooped it up very quickly. That quarter burned my palm, because I was afraid someone might have seen me after all. When I went back to class, every time someone came through the classroom door, I thought the person was coming to point a finger at me. The fear of having that quarter in my possession that day overrode my anxiety of being in school.

I didn't tell my father about the quarter, because I believed he would have made me return it to the exact spot where I'd found it. I was well out of school before I ever mentioned that incident.

The teachers gave us assigned seats, off to the side, in the back of the room, so that we would not be able to intermingle. We were told that the seating arrangements were for our own protection. The atmosphere in the classroom was unbelievable—faces full of hatred and nonacceptance. Most of the teachers never talked *to* us just *at* us. I was never called upon to speak out loud, which made me feel more rejected than selected. I could give no input into the classes; I could offer no opinions of my own; I couldn't answer any of the teachers' questions by raising my hand because I was just going to be ignored. On the one hand, I felt invisible, unheard, and nonexistent. On the other hand, I was a little relieved because I felt any acknowledgment of my existence was going to be negative.

To protect myself from the pain of rejection, humiliation, and disrespect, I responded to most situations with a resiliency and toughness that might have seemed impressive to some, but only I knew my demeanor was very deceptive.

I shared the same fears, desires, and challenges as white students in terms of trying to earn an education, but the white students came to school and had the pleasure of concentrating on learning. Black students like me had the stress of trying to deal with the negative, racial issues on a daily basis, and at the same time, trying to work toward a good education. Facing those slurs and hateful stares from the students and some of the teachers made me burn with an inner rage about the injustices inflicted upon me because of the color of my skin.

There were plenty of signs that read, "Niggers Go Home," and "2, 4, 6, 8 . . . We don't want to integrate!" A few white students, a very few, simply left us alone. Some just stared sullenly or curiously or hatefully. The white kids who acted as though they wanted to talk to us were afraid to because they knew if they were caught, they would be teased and called "nigger lovers."

On a rare occasion, I'd find a calm moment to sort things out in my own mind, and I'd imagine myself up on the ceiling, looking down on the sea of white heads with a mere sprinkling of black heads scurrying about among them. From atop, everything seemed normal, but once my consciousness flowed down to join the crowd, things became as they were, voices swarming around me, taunting. The other black students and I moved as quickly as possible when going from class to class. Those day-to-day confrontations drained the energy from me that should have been used for learning.

I was amazed by the speed at which I grew to despise that place. The hatred grew and swelled even stronger each day until it seemed to swirl around me like the air I breathed. Sometimes, I felt as though I might choke with so much hatred boiling inside me. I had never before heard the word *nigger* used so much in my life. Fortunately, I had been taught that it was a word that defined those who used it, not those whom it was used against, and that particular word, I knew, didn't apply to me. But one big, tall, blonde girl with a bouffant hairstyle called me a nigger each time she saw me in the hallway, never saying anything else, just that one word. I tried to ignore her, remembering the "no violence" rule. I often wondered, though, what she would do if I called her a nigger back.

One day as we passed in the hall and she was about to hiss "Nigger," I was ready for her. As she neared me, I hissed "Nigger" at her before she had time to say anything or react to what I'd said. She stopped dead still in her tracks, astonished. She looked utterly perplexed, for it took her a moment to digest what I had called her. The expression on her face was that of complete disbelief as she ran down the hall screaming to anyone who would listen that I called her a nigger. I was rather surprised to see her reaction, but was also very pleased at the same time. She never bothered me again. I couldn't help but smirk every time I saw her after that.

I learned to progress from shock to survival. I never did get used to the insults and the constant stares, but I did learn how to deal with them. Now that I look back, it was funny to see the white kids sliding along the walls of the hall, hugging them to the nth degree, whenever they saw one of us black kids coming. They were very careful not to touch us; I suppose they still believed that the black would rub off.

The black students in my class congregated at recess or any free time we had together to talk and share the events of the day—the complexity of being black students in this privileged white world, the conflicting pulls on us from the world we were thrust into and trying to become a part of, and the world where we had once felt safe and secure.

The topic "How can we find our own true identities?" was constantly argued and discussed among the ten of us. During the school hours, with the strangeness of the white attitudes, the outright meanness of the students, the general disrespect for other human beings that was displayed, I felt I was transported every day into a foreign world, and it was only after school that I could let my guard down and be myself.

Attending school with the white kids caused me to grow curious about them as well and about their world in which they seemingly ruled everything and everyone as if by some invisible remote control. Were they naturally meaner and stronger? What made it necessary for them to treat others so badly? Where did all that anger and hatred come from?

What made them tick? That year filled me full of questions for which there were no easy answers.

Lee and I were still dating. He never tried to discourage me, in any way, from continuing to go to Jefferson High. It was understood that since my father agreed with the Liddell High administration that I should go, then it was a done deal and not to be interfered with. He usually waited for me in the evenings to get off the transport bus to walk me to my home bus. It was during those walks when Lee often asked how I was being treated. He wanted to know the names of some of the kids in my class, because he knew some who lived near him in Red Lick, a small community about twelve miles north of Fayette. It was closer to the Claiborne County line. When I gave him the names of some of my classmates, he assured me that the kids he knew, who lived near him, would not be bothering me in any way. That gesture endeared him more to me, because it made me feel some small sense of protection.

At the white school rules and regulations were strict, and pink slips were issued if we disobeyed any of those rules. If a student received more than three pink slips, that was grounds for dismissal. I don't know if the pink slip rule had always been a part of the school rules or if that was one more rule created to keep us in our place.

I did receive more than three pink slips, but I wasn't dismissed. I got into a couple of scrapes with Marilyn Nations, a girl from my library class. As was the case with the big blonde girl with the bouffant hair, she liked harassing me also. She had a habit of sitting in my assigned seat at the library table. She'd always sit there and wait until the last minute prior to the teacher entering before getting up, knowing that if I was caught standing, I'd get into trouble. I tried to ignore her and simply stood behind my seat until she decided to get out of it. I was barely able to sit down in time before Mrs. Meyers, the librarian, entered the room.

One day as I entered the library, I saw Marilyn perched in my seat. She was talking across the table to some of her friends as if I was invisible. Having had enough of this ridiculous behavior, I walked up to her, grabbed the collar of her shirt, and pulled her out of my seat. She jumped up, ran to the office, and reported me to the principal. Immediately, I was called to the office, where Mr. Gavin told me to sit down and tell him what had happened. After my explanation, he said, "Well, Martha, rules are rules, and you will have to be written up for your behavior."

I'm not sure if Marilyn was written up or not, but that was my first pink slip. Once again, the incident had to be reported to Mr. Berry at Liddell High, and once again, he tried to explain to me that I had to stay strong and ignore any racial incidents, as well as any racial slurs. This time I felt anger toward his words of wisdom, for he didn't have to endure the draining, hateful confrontations day after day.

Marilyn just wouldn't give up. She continued to ignore me, sitting in my chair whenever she felt like it. After another week of this behavior, I knew I had to put an end to this madness somehow. I was faced with an extreme situation; therefore, my remedy had to also be extreme.

The very next day as I walked into the library, I saw her sitting in my seat as usual, leaning over talking with her friends. As usual, she ignored me as I neared my table. I decisively walked up to her and pushed the chair into the table with her sitting in it. She screamed in pain or surprise, I'm not sure which. When I released the chair, she jumped up and ran out of the library and straight into Mr. Gavin's office.

Again, I was called in and issued another pink slip. Again,

Mr. Gavin went over the rules and regulations, but as he was talking this time, his demeanor was a little different. His tone as he talked to me sounded softer. He seemed genuinely concerned and was talking to me, not at me.

He said, "Martha, explain to me in your own words what just happened in the library. This is the second time you and Marilyn Nations have had an incident in less than two weeks."

I sat there, very nervously, and tried to explain exactly what Marilyn did and how it all got started. I told him that this behavior had gone on for over two weeks, and I knew something needed to be done.

He interrupted me and asked, "Why didn't you report these incidents to the librarian?"

"Well, I didn't know how I was going to be able to prove it even if I had told her, because Mrs. Meyers never actually saw Marilyn out of her seat. By the time she came in and got to her desk, everyone was sitting in their rightful seats. She never saw me standing and waiting." I also told him that I had tried talking to Marilyn, but she just ignored me as if I wasn't there. She'd just continue to talk with her friends. In the end, I told him how humiliated I felt just standing and waiting each time I entered the library. All the others found their seats; why couldn't she find hers?

After my explanation, he said he understood that I was just trying to defend myself. Mr. Gavin nicknamed me the "little rebel," and said I was a force to be reckoned with. "You may be little," he said, "but you surely mean to be heard!"

For once, I sensed that I finally had one of the school's officials on my side. That feeling didn't make going to school there any easier, but it did take the edge off for that day.

I grew tired of constantly feeling beaten and of having to return, five days in a row, for more. I grew tired of being called a nigger. I grew tired of the stares. Even though I felt that violence was a perverted way of life, I decided that it was, sometimes, a very necessary tactic and technique.

However, I did learn one thing from the people at that school—that I could never love my enemy. Because I didn't want to disappoint our educational leaders, especially Mrs. Knox, for whom I had the deepest respect, I tried to refrain from fighting back. On the other hand, my father had taught me not only to be proud, but also to defend myself against any kind of assault, whether it was physical or verbal. I was taught to never turn the other cheek. If I had to go to school with those people, then I would refuse to let them see any weakness or fear in me.

The prom was canceled that year. Jefferson High School officials decided that there would be no prom, because intermingling might lead to something else, maybe dating between the races or even worse, marriage. We were never invited to attend any school functions; the PTA meetings were even held in private session, excluding all black parents.

Saturday was traditionally the big shopping day for blacks in the South, the day when, their work finally done for the week, blacks poured into the downtown area, both to shop and to socialize. When I was still a senior in high school in 1968, a café was located on Main Street called Porter's Café. Despite the fact that the stores by that time had been integrated, some of the privately owned businesses were very slow in taking down their demeaning signs and on Porter's front door hung a sign that read "Whites Only." In the back of the café, around the side with a separate entrance, was a door with a sign that read "Colored."

Porter's Café was privately owned by the Porter family, and they didn't feel they had to abide by the new integration laws no matter who said they should. Porter's was also a place where people went to eat. I had seen many black women and men disappear through that "Colored" door and stay for hours. My stepmother had been one of those people. I had always wanted to go inside that place and see for myself what went on that kept those women and men inside for such a long time.

One day, my fellow classmate Bob and I sneaked away from school and went uptown to exercise our so-called rights. Someone had given us a button with a black hand grasping a white hand and had dared us to wear it. After we left school, I pinned the button on my blouse and wore it bravely. Bob and I walked downtown to Porter's Café, walked right up to the front door, looked at each other for support, and went in. We were very scared, but it was too late to turn around. As we entered, a big burly white man stood towering over us and said in his most intimidating voice, "What are you doing coming in here? We don't serve no niggers!"

His words conjured up the punch line of a joke I'd heard somewhere in the past. I hadn't understood the joke at the time, but the punch line seemed right for the moment. I looked up at him and said in a very timid, squeaky voice, "And we don't eat no niggers!" Then we turned and quickly walked out, afraid that the big burly man would follow us out to the street. Even if those people had served us, we didn't have the six cents between the two of us to buy a soda pop.

When we were out on the street away from that place, Bob and I looked at each other and burst out laughing at the foolish thing we had done. Days later, it was still hard for us to believe that we had actually done such a thing. Needless to say, we never told our parents about our adventure.

Throughout my education, I had always been an above-average student, but my grades were slowly slipping from As to Cs. I just couldn't put all I needed into my studies to maintain an A average because I was forced to concentrate more on survival than on my studies. My father didn't scold or punish me for the drop in my grades because, he told me later, he thought I was being punished enough by the school system.

Instead of studying, I had to constantly think of ways to retaliate, ways to get even, and methods to prepare myself for the next day's events, whatever they might be. I went home at night and consulted with the other students to find out how their day went and what strategies we could use the following day. I felt we had to stay a step ahead, and I decided it would be up to me to plan what step that would be. And, of course, I was still seeing Lee.

During my one year at Jefferson High School, aside from the hateful stares, the taunting, and the forced conversations, we still had little contact with the white race. In many ways, segregation still ruled. No special efforts were made by the faculty to establish any kind of real contact between the races.

I discovered something else about myself while attending school with the white students: my own true feelings toward racism. The extraordinary cultural differences between the races had a profound and psychological effect on me. It instilled in me a stronger sense of identity.

I grew up in a home in which there were no prejudices. The only thing I knew about white people before going to school with them was that they were a different color. My father had taught me that no one was better than me. Conversely, the white kids had been taught differently. I often wondered how those students learned to hate so deeply and at such a young age. After that year, I hated all white people just as blindly and viciously as they hated blacks.

The nine months I spent at Jefferson High were the longest nine months of my life. Never before had I looked forward to the ending of a school year as I did that year. The older black folks whom I encountered praised me lavishly for what I was doing. They always greeted me with, "God bless you, chile," and would proceed to tell me how brave I was. They slowly shook my hand, holding on much longer than necessary. I felt anything but brave.

I never really understood why I didn't just simply give it up and go back to my own school; there were many times I wanted to. Obviously, something deep inside me must have enjoyed dealing with the challenges I faced. One thing for sure, if I was ever going to make sense of all of this, then I knew I had to lead my own struggle for salvation and find my own strength within myself. If what our educational leaders had told us in those preparation-for-Jefferson-High sessions were true, then this would all be worth it someday.

Figure 3. Advertisement after desegregation

3
First Marriage

Lee didn't seem to have a serious bone in his body; everything was strictly fun for him. Perhaps that's one of the reasons I clung to him during my traumatic last year in school. My life at Jefferson High was anything but humorous, and Lee's sense of humor helped me keep my sanity. I knew that was one of the qualities I liked about him, but I also knew that we needed more than that on which to build a solid relationship.

Right after high school, Lee relentlessly and constantly pestered me to marry him. I didn't quite know how to say no to him and mean it. Back then, if a girl didn't go to college right after high school, marriage was the usual alternative.

The closer we got to the wedding date, the more eager he seemed and the more reluctant I was, but I didn't see any way out of the dilemma. Lee and I were married shortly after our high school graduation in May 1968, despite the fact that on my wedding day, Daddy pulled me aside and looked me straight in my eyes and said, "Tootise, I know you feel as though you want to eat that boy up, but before this marriage is over, you're gonna wish you had, mark my words."

Those words stayed with me during the ceremony and all through the four and a half years of my marriage to Lee. It didn't take long before I realized I should have listened to my father. Although he wasn't an educated man, Daddy had great insight and was very wise about life in general. Had I eaten Lee up for the first main meal, I would have spared us both the miserable life we shared.

Daddy had agreed that we would live with him and Louberta until we were able to afford a place, but when Louberta found out, she took her great-aunt and -uncle and moved out, back into their old house, which was about a mile and a half from ours. I breathed a sigh of relief knowing Lee wouldn't have to put up with what my sister and I had for almost three years. With the three of them gone, our living conditions improved somewhat. Louetta, Lee, and I had the house most of the time to ourselves. Daddy spent the days and most nights with his wife, giving Lee and me his bedroom.

Lee was working at odd jobs here and there when we got married, which paid for some of the necessities and bought a bit of gas for the car, but very little else. We had a very productive garden at Daddy's house, which is where most of our food came from. Life was simple, getting by day to day, with no thoughts toward the future.

I became pregnant immediately. We had never discussed having children. It happened, and as far as I was concerned, it was just part of being married. The upcoming birth of our first child prompted Lee to apply to the Mississippi Corps of Engineers, and he was hired at once as a general laborer, but the job took him away from home and as my due date neared, Lee began to dread the fact that he might not be home when the baby was born. I'm sure there was some truth in that, but it was also a way to get out of going to work because once the baby was born, he never went back.

It didn't take very long for my father's prediction about Lee's and my marriage to come true. By the time I was seven months pregnant, the humor and wit that I found so appealing in Lee when we first met was no longer there. The fun side of him had disappeared and in its place a dark side emerged which I hadn't known existed.

After the baby was born I felt overwhelmed and very emotional. I had gone to hospital thinking I was having a boy and I was going to name my son Stephen Demetris. I never gave any thought to having a girl. My mother-in-law and a few other older neighbors had convinced me that I was carrying a boy because my stomach hung very low, an old wives' tale, but my mother-in-law had already had ten children, so I believed she surely knew what she was talking about.

For the life of me, I couldn't come up with a single name for my little bundle of joy, until I found an article in *Ebony* magazine written about the Supremes. Florence Ballard, one of the singers in the famous girl group, had named one of her twins Nichole Renee. That name sounded good to me, so my firstborn had her name.

Lee rationalized quitting his job by claiming he wanted to find something in the area that would allow him to come home every day and spend more time being a father, but we needed a steady income more than we needed to spend so much time together. I could see, day by day, his anger and hostility growing toward me. He only seemed happy when he was holding and playing with his little girl. He became obsessive about controlling my every move.

We had a good baby, healthy, happy, and very outgoing, but as time went on I began to feel even more closed in and smothered, increasingly depressed. No one in my family suspected how I was feeling. We weren't raised to talk about such things, and my girlfriend Bob was the only person I would have shared those feelings with, but by then she had married and moved to Waukegan, Illinois.

Elsewhere in Fayette, things were changing dramatically

because Charles Evers, brother of slain civil rights leader Medgar Evers, had come to the area earlier in the 1960s, and decided to run for mayor of our town in 1969, bringing with him a new era.

Charles Evers had taken over Medgar Evers's post as head of the NAACP in Mississippi after his brother was killed, even though he always thought he could better fulfill Medgar's obligations to the people in civil rights and in business than he could in politics. He said he felt that taking the post was what Medgar would have wanted. In 1968, he was asked to run for Congress from the state's third district.

Later, in speech after speech explaining his decision, he told us that the impetus to run came from a little old lady sitting beside him at one of his NAACP meetings who looked up at him and said, "Mr. Evers, we have done everything you have ever asked of us to do. We have gone to jail for you, we've marched with you, we picketed with you, and we have boycotted for you. Now, we are asking you to do one thing for us, and you want to refuse." After that, he said he took a leave of absence from his post as field director of the Mississippi chapter of the NAACP to run.

Seven candidates ran in the special primary in 1968. Six of them were white. The seventh was Charles Evers. For the first time in history, voters were faced with a black candidate who had to be taken seriously. Also for the first time in recent history, Mississippi had developed a politician who combined a clear political philosophy with tremendous energy and magnetic personal appeal.

The local paper quoted an article by Robert Canzoneri printed in *Harper's Magazine* that said the Evers charm was as different from the Kennedy charm as Mississippi black was from Boston Irish, but it was strikingly similar in its force. He had a desire to build a sound economy, to establish an honorable working relationship, and to build some unity between the races. Evers lost handily in that congressional race, but his appetite for political office had been whetted and Fayette, Mississippi, with its majority black population looked very appealing.

One of the first things Evers did when he came to Fayette was to organize an NAACP (National Association for the Advancement of Colored People) branch, which took in members by the hundreds.

I didn't follow Charles Evers's political career closely in the beginning because Lee forbade me to go to town alone, although he was rarely home. Many times I wanted to sneak into town to see what all the buzz was about surrounding Charles Evers, but I was always afraid someone might see me and tell Lee. As Evers made headlines all across America, however, the townspeople, I among them, had to stand up and take notice. After I was married, I was considered old enough to attend mass meetings if I wanted to, and I sometimes went with my father. I did see Evers at a distance during one of those mass meetings and heard him talking about running for mayor of Fayette. I remember our neighbor, Mr. Vest, leaning over to my father and saying, "Pee, chile, they messin' with them white folks, ain't they? Gonna get them white folks outta office, jest you wait and see. What do you think ole R. J. Allen [the current mayor] will have to say about this? Boy, I never thought I'd live to see this!"

As I've said, my father was a soft-spoken man, which only added emphasis to his words when he said, "Yeah, can't wait to see them bastards outta office. It's about time for R. J. Allen to get out. He's been there forever and never done a thing for colored people but gave them turnips greens. I never took any from 'em because I raised my own greens."

1969 statistics offer some understanding of the grim situation in our town before Charles Evers came: forty-five percent of the total population, including about two-thirds of the black population, was on welfare. Fayette, Jefferson County, was the seat of the fourth poorest county in America. Annual per capita income was about one thousand dollars, one-third of the national average. Virtually no industry operated within Fayette, and our town had the second-highest unemployment rate in the state. Since more than three-fourths of the county's population was black, and since the distribution of money was extremely uneven, with whites enjoying a much larger share, the severity of black poverty in the county was actually greater than anywhere else. The average level of education for blacks was fifth grade.

Fayette had only two white doctors that served the entire Jefferson County population of ten thousand. The school system accepted the rule of integration, but was still under the control of white segregationists. As a result, the town was forfeiting vast sums of federal funds. Talk about cutting off your nose to spite your face!

Except for the white neighborhoods in Fayette, no adequate sewage system or water supply existed. What passed for public recreation facilities—a swimming pool and a playground—had been closed four years earlier to avoid federal court requirements for integration. It was hell all over Mississippi, but more so in Fayette, because of such strong opposition by the white people. Coupled with the abject poverty were three centuries of unrelenting racial oppression, which consistently denied black Mississippians the fruits of the American dream.

In the spring of 1969, Mr. Evers publicly announced his candidacy for mayor of Fayette, running against Mayor R. J. "Turnip Green" Allen, who had held the office for eighteen years. The nickname "Turnip Green" came from the fact that he gave out turnip greens at election time to those few blacks who were registered to vote. Mr. Evers announced that a complete economic boycott would be waged against the white merchants, and not a black cent would be spent in any white-owned business until a list of black demands was met. Such tactics had proven highly profitable for black storeowners in the past.

The three department stores in town, all owned by white people, were boycotted by the blacks, along with the two grocery stores. Since the town was about eighty-five percent black, the boycotts seriously hurt the white business owners. Blacks, most often, bought on credit and paid up their bills once crops were harvested, so long-term white storeowners knew their revenues for the year would be seriously decreased. Even though black sharecroppers feared the white storeowners might "call in" the credit owed, they hesitantly went along with the boycotts.

Evers, being a shrewd businessman himself, did very well with a food store he purchased during the boycott, which he named Evers Grocery Store, on the lower south side of Fayette. He didn't necessarily offer credit to customers. He taught them to pay as you go and not to rely so heavily on credit, which had kept them beholden to white storeowners in the past. He told us the only way to freedom was not to "owe anybody anything." I suppose that's why many blacks today remain so opposed to putting their money into banks; why let someone else profit off your money when you can take care of it yourself?

When Mr. Evers wasn't organizing boycotts or attending mass meetings, he was out shaking hands with the people in the community, becoming better acquainted with them, and thus letting them get better acquainted with him. By doing this, he also gained much of their trust and respect.

He was overwhelmed with black political help, for his presence had attracted nationwide press interest in such newspapers as the *Washington Post*, the *Chicago Tribune*, and the *New York Times* just to name a few. He told the people that our hardships would soon be behind us as we moved forward in this new era. According to Evers, we blacks were going to receive a square deal at last.

We could see evidence that the white resistance was crumbling fast when some of the white merchants approached the black community's most respectable leaders with their pleas to end the boycotts. They told the leaders that we black people should not let an outside agitator come in and tell us what to do and how to live our lives. We had always lived in "a peaceful community," the merchants insisted. But the blacks continued to support the boycotts. We had already silently proclaimed our leader.

Charles Evers became mayor of Fayette on May 13, 1969. I was not eligible to vote in that election (the voting age wasn't lowered to eighteen until 1971 by the 26th Amendment) but I remember people coming around, trying to get every black person in town to register and vote. Pamphlets were distributed to potential voters, outlining the deadlines for registration and requirements of eligibility. The pamphlet, published by the Voter Education Project in Atlanta and the Mississippi Center for Elected Officials in Tougaloo, Mississippi, proclaimed:

You can register if:
You have lived in the state and county for one
year by the time of the election.
You have lived in your voting district for six
months by the time of the election.
You are 21 years old by the time of the election. If

you are 18, 19 or 20 years old, you can register now, but you can't vote until the 1972 election.

You have not been convicted in Mississippi of: murder, rape, bribery, theft, arson, obtaining money or goods under false pretense, perjury, forgery, embezzlement, bigamy. If you were convicted of any of these crimes in a Federal Court or in another state, you can still register in Mississippi.

YOU ARE NEVER TOO OLD TO REGISTER

If you are under 21 years old, the clerk may require you to show some form of identification. When you go to register, take with you a birth certificate, a draft card, a family Bible, a school record, or some other form of identification which will prove your age.

YOU DO NOT HAVE TO BE ABLE TO READ OR WRITE!

YOU DO NOT HAVE TO PAY A POLL TAX!

My father at some point proudly registered and voted (even though he couldn't read or write) and bragged about it to Mr. Vest. "Vest, you registered yet?" he asked.

Mr. Vest replied, "No, Pee, can we go now and do it? If we can, how do we go about doing it?"

My father again stated proudly, "Jest go to the courthouse and tell them you want to register to vote. They will give you a paper to sign. If you can't read or write just mark your x on the line." They could hardly believe it was possible for a black man to become mayor, but were fired up about the possibility of it happening. (By the time reelection came around, all of my family had registered, including me.) I think most blacks were fired up about the possibility, but, like me, weren't afraid, just reluctant. I didn't quite understand why a black man would even try running against a white man. However, from what I had read about Evers in the local newspaper and what I had heard about him from other people around town that possibility could very well become a reality. Mr. Evers was the closest thing to a celebrity that had ever set foot in Fayette.

Charles Evers said that Mississippi was different from any other state in the nation. Despite the hate, the harassment, the intimidation, and denial of basic human rights for blacks, there was still something about the state that was lovable. He told us there was something about the relationship between the mean white people and the scary Negroes that didn't exist anywhere else, a closeness between the Mississippi whites and blacks that could be found in no other state. He said he couldn't explain it, but he knew when he went around campaigning for mayor, some blacks would, inevitably, vote for his white opponent. Some blacks believed, like most whites, that the office of mayor should be filled by a white man, and it was hard for them to comprehend differently. Evers said: "Fayette is our Israel; I am determined to be mayor of all the people, not just the black people." Blacks had even nicknamed him "Moses of Mississippi," ready to lead us to the Promised Land. Others, however, called him a "money-hungry, power-crazy demon."

Charles Evers defeated "Turnip Green" Allen by 128 votes. Some white merchants fled the city after the election, selling their businesses and their homes, refusing to live under the leadership of a black mayor, many of them in fear for their lives because they had so maliciously maligned blacks for years. Porter's Café, the place I'd ventured into with my friend during high school that had a "colored" entrance and a "white" entrance, posted a sign that read: "Every cent spent by a nigger will be donated to the Ku Klux Klan." Soon after Evers got elected, Porter's closed its doors and left. The outgoing mayor and his aldermen emptied the city funds, leaving the city virtually bankrupt, and the majority of white city employees resigned after the election.

The first time I saw Mayor Evers up close, he was getting ready to deliver his inaugural speech on July 7, 1969. I was completely mesmerized. The whole town was invited. This tall, slightly heavy, bronze-skinned man had great charisma. A curious quality of delight emanated from him as well as a vast amount of warmth, which almost, though not quite, erased a stolid and reserved watchfulness with which he confronted the crowd. When he walked onto that platform to address the audience, his mere presence commanded respect and dignity. According to Charlie Vess's article about the parade in the *Fayette Chronicle* the next day, about thirty-five whites showed up.

Summers in Mississippi are very hot and humid, but still, every person I could see was dressed in his or her Sunday best. The older black women were dressed in hats and gloves, high heels, and stockings. The men were all in white shirts and ties, some with jackets on and some with their jackets slung over their shoulders perspiring to the nth degree. Each person wanted to look his very best for our newly elected mayor. Due to my limited wardrobe, I wore my one and only good dress, a straight, navy-blue minidress, and a pair of flat shoes. Since I'd just delivered Nikki in April, the old womenfolks told me not to wear shoes with a high heel, not that I had any, for fear of hurting my lower abdomen from standing too long. Back then, old folks had plenty of myths and superstitions about any condition of the body, but probably that was good advice.

Lee was at the parade with me, as was my whole family, but I'd left Nikki with her paternal grandmother, the weather being extremely hot and humid for a newborn. Lee's family lived near the Claiborne County line and didn't bother much with any happenings in Jefferson County, so Lee, his father, and one of Lee's brothers were the extent of his family's attendance.

The crowd waited patiently for the start of this event, the sun sending down rays of heat with virtually no breeze stirring to cool the people off. Women, using their best Sunday-go-to- meetin' hankies, mopped away the endless downpour of perspiration. The excitement of waiting to hear the mayor's speech was much more important than worrying about being uncomfortable in the heat.

People were gathered in groups, laughing, talking, and having a good ole time despite the heat. Many of the women fanned themselves with small cardboard-like fans with thin wooden sticks stapled to the back for handles, just like the fans I used as a child, but these had different advertisements. The front of these fans bore the faces of Martin Luther King, Jr., John F. Kennedy, and Robert Kennedy. People were scattered all up and down Main Street, but most were gathered in the center of town where the ceremonies were about to take place.

Four new shiny police cars with flashing red lights came cruising down the street, indicating the beginning of the parade. The first float that was carrying the new mayor and his celebrity friends was decorated in red, white, and blue, representing Jefferson County's rebirth to America. Pulling the float was a car that displayed two large American flags, one on each side in front. Huge poster boards attached to the doors proclaimed, "Our Newly Elected Mayor: Charles Evers." Next, a patrol car followed with two black policemen inside. The rest of the cars and floats followed closely behind, including floats from the local college, Alcorn State University, and our high school, Liddell High. Alcorn's school colors, purple and gold, adorned their float, which carried the professors and the performing band. Our high school colors were similar—blue and gold—but of course, the style of decorations was different. Our high school band gave just as great a performance as the college band, and the music in the air seemed to reverberate right through the crowd.

As the float carrying the mayor passed by, the people were waving and chanting, "Mayor Evers, Mayor Evers, Mayor Evers." The excitement was contagious as everyone began waving and chanting in tune. One of the floats had a pair of scales on it. The two pans were labeled "Justice" and "Equality," and in the center on top of the scales were the words "For All."

The parade moved slowly through the heat waves radiating off Main Street. The temperature was over a hundred degrees that day with the sun mercilessly beaming down upon us. I could see the beads of sweat popping out on the faces of the people around me as soon as they were wiped off again.

The mile-long parade had formed on the south edge of town, past the Medgar Evers Shopping Center about 10:30 that morning, and it lasted for hours. I had never seen so many colorful floats, decorated cars, or people in a parade before in Fayette. We had local Boy Scouts and some troops from other towns, all carrying the American flag. A green Chevy pickup truck carried a band, playing tubas, saxophones, and a number of African drums. Right behind the green Chevy pickup marched Ramsey Clark, the former attorney general of the United States. Clark served under President Lyndon B. Johnson from 1967 to 1969. I had never witnessed so many VIPs in our little town and all because we had a new black mayor. I nearly had to pinch myself to believe it was all real, to believe that I was so close to so many important people. The citizens of Jefferson County witnessed history that day.

The parade ended in a lot behind the town hall where the

inauguration was to take place. Even though the crowd was mostly black, a few local, white merchants were standing among them, curiously looking on.

We'd been told that well-known liberals and other dignitaries were coming, and I had no idea who these famous people were on the podium, but the program handout listed them as: Ramsey Clark, Shirley MacLaine, Whitney Young, Paul O'Dwyer, Theodore Sorensen, and Julian Bond (all of whom were wiping sweat from their bodies as they awaited Evers's entrance).

It seemed to me like the whole town of Fayette was one big television screen that day. I was so excited all I could do was keep my eyes glued to the spot on the platform where the new mayor was to appear. This was the most moving and impressive event I had ever had the pleasure of witnessing. During the wait, some of the boards used for the platform on which the ceremonies were to be held gave way due to the weight of so many dignitaries. Some of Mayor Evers's security people nailed the boards back together; it wasn't much of an interruption, and the ceremony kept going.

Finally, the inauguration got under way. The master of ceremonies was Dr. Aaron Henry, a pharmacist, who was also the head of the NAACP in the state of Mississippi. He was known as one of the most respected civil rights activists in the state. When he took the platform, he called out to the noisy crowd, "This is some black power!"

The crowd screamed back, "Black power, black power, black power."

Several minutes passed before the people calmed down. Dr. Henry went on to introduce the Reverend William J. Morrissey, SSJ, chaplain of the Adams County chapter of the NAACP, who gave the invocation. He prayed, "Holy Father, today we stand before you, facing a new era." Leontyne Price, a native Mississippian, sang "The Star-Spangled Banner." I never thought I'd see the woman who made Broadway history, playing in *Porgy and Bess*, in Fayette.

Next, the justice of the peace, Willie Thompson, swore in the five members of the board of aldermen and Evers as new members of the election commission. Then he swore in the new mayor. The applause was like heavy bolts of thunder. An infectious feeling of pride swept through the crowd back on that hot, humid, July day in 1969. Yes, a new era had, indeed, begun.

The new mayor stepped forward to deliver his inaugural speech. At last, the moment everyone had been waiting for. The crowd, which had been quietly murmuring, settled down. The first thing he talked about was the collapsing of the platform earlier. He joked that if the white people had been the kind of people that we thought they were, the platform wouldn't have accidentally fallen; it would have been torn down the night before. That statement drew lots of bobbing of the heads, back and forth from the people in the crowd agreeing with the mayor.

Mayor Evers began his speech. "To those who have walked with me, and to those who have gone to jail with me, all of you who have helped make this day possible, I say thank you, first of all."

He also told the crowd his feelings about his white brothers. He said, "However you may feel about our white brothers, we got to understand one thing; they just don't know any better. We're not going to do to them what they did to us, but we are going to make damn sure that they don't do us no more." He emphasized that he would be a "law and order" mayor, by which he meant that the law would be enforced evenhandedly and firmly toward all citizens, regardless of race.

After that short introduction to his speech, the crowd went wild again with applause. Each time, it took several minutes to settle everyone down. We all joined hands as the mayor told us we had to try and bury all the hatred and the evils of the past. We had to look forward to the future and make this county and all of Mississippi a clean and righteous place for all of us to live in. As I listened to him speak, I knew he had given us a new purpose in life, a purpose to survive and overcome all the obstacles that had held us down for so many years. For the first time in modern-day history, the black citizens no longer had to be afraid for their lives or their property as a result of arbitrary police action.

I watched all the faces around me being transformed with hope and courage. The feelings caused by that experience are hard to put into words. That sense of hope was so strong, so pervasive, that each of us felt with complete certainty that there *could* be, that there *would* be, a better world and a good life ahead for us if we worked hard enough for it.

At the conclusion of the ceremonies, there was a buffet luncheon in that old Confederate Memorial Park, the park that had always been exclusively for whites, and a barbecue at the Medgar Evers Shopping Center. Most people attended both events talking, enjoying themselves, walking around, and trying to digest the day's events. I heard comments throughout the crowd like "Chile, I never thought I'd live to see this day" and "I'm still having a hard time believing this."

It was breathtaking.

Somewhere I read that there were two types of hospitality traditions in the South: black hospitality and white hospitality. They had almost nothing to do with each other, except that it was the black people who cooked the food that the white people served to their friends. But that day, the black people cooked the food that was served to all who were in attendance. Now was the time to start some new traditions.

"It doesn't matter who the mayor is," I heard one local white merchant say, "once a man has been elected, he deserves the respect of all the citizens." He knew as well as the blacks that Mayor Evers would do for that town what no one had ever done before him, and not just for the black people, but also for the remaining white people who had stayed behind as well.

Some of the businessmen stated that Fayette was badly in need of industry, but creating a climate to attract that industry was going to be a more difficult undertaking than might be generally assumed. Fayette was located near two highways and the river. It was on the railroad line, which made for an excellent location to attract some type of industry, but the white businessmen still wondered if the new mayor could do it. The black people had little or no doubt that the mayor, with his national connections, could persuade some big firms to move in. They had little doubt that he could do anything he said he could. Once this happened, you could bet the white people would not be criticizing him then.

Of all the necessities of life, which most Americans took for granted, the most critically lacking in Fayette was a modern medical facility. The trustees of the Medgar Evers Fund had voted to allocate up to $100,000 to construct a new and sorely needed community health center for Fayette. Literally no facilities for the care of our people existed. The elderly had no place to go for medical help, and the children were without daycare centers. There were no Head Start centers in our area at that time. There was no facility to help the young working mothers. That duty fell to grandparents or other relatives.

When built, the center alone would create hundreds of jobs for Jefferson County citizens. Mayor Evers had also contracted for a subsidiary of the International Telephone and Telegraph Corporation to produce auto parts in the area. That factory was later known as ITT.

The new 25,000-square-foot, single-story building was built in four months by a syndicate of white residents at a small cost. At the ribbon cutting ceremony, the mayor commented on the breakthrough that we had made. He then told the citizens of another factory that might be coming soon. He was in the middle of negotiations with a biracial firm from Jackson to put in a chemical plant.

We, the people of Fayette, Mississippi, could not have been more pleased with the progress of our town in such a short time. Even the remaining white people had to grudgingly admit that the black government was bringing a new vitality to the sleepy little town. The business community showed signs of renewed activity shortly after Evers took office. The *Fayette Experience*, as the new mayor referred to it, symbolized the changing of attitudes of both blacks and whites.

But the changes definitely didn't happen overnight. When I was in town with Nikki one day, I stopped at the Confederate Memorial Park across from the courthouse, the park with the statue of a Confederate soldier leaning on his rifle that I'd stared at from a distance as a child because it was "whites only." I smiled as I sat down on a bench to rest with my baby girl for a while . . . just because I now could, and it felt good. One year before, I would never have dreamed of sitting on that park bench, would never have tried. I had passed by that bench so often during my childhood, knowing that something terrible would happen to me if a white person caught me sitting there. To have the simple pleasure of sitting on a park bench, just like any other human being, filled me with hope. I must have closed my eyes to treasure the moment, for I was startled to hear an old, white male voice say, "Nigger, get off this bench." Since it had always been ingrained in me to never disrespect the elderly, I just stared up at him. I didn't move. I knew I was no nigger. And I didn't have to move. That old gentleman slowly walked off, muttering under his breath.

Mayor Evers gave most of his attention to the economy of Fayette. While the town was beginning to show signs of progress, the mayor still had many new problems to face. A month after taking office, he discovered that only two of the twelve construction workers who were hired to build the medical building were black, although the original contract stipulated a more equitable racial mix. This didn't go over too well. In the end, more blacks were hired to complete what became the Medgar Evers Comprehensive Health Center.

He knew most Fayette citizens received lower welfare payments than in any other state, but he made it very clear that he only believed in welfare as a means to an end. He never wanted welfare for his people; he wanted workfare. Mayor Evers gave us great pride in our town and in ourselves as well. For the first time, our local government was not attempting to exact privileges and power for one race at the expense of the other race. He made us aware of the battles that were being fought all over the state for racial equality. Mayor Evers knew how to utilize each and every opportunity that came his way. Fayette became a great example of integration, and it felt good to be able to walk down Main Street and not have to see the standard "Colored" and "Whites Only" signs hanging on local business doors.

By the end of 1969, Fayette was showing signs of great

change. The people had listened to what the mayor had said. We didn't vote for the black man or the white man; we, indeed, voted for the best man. Mayor Evers's inauguration had brought about immediate and sweeping changes to the town and in the attitudes of the local businessmen.

Black cashiers worked in all of the downtown stores and were no longer limited to just cleaning them. Now we had some black-owned businesses in the mix. Black and white doctors from different parts of the United States were coming in to be a part of this movement and to work at the new health center. For the first time, a black physician from a neighboring county, Dr. Charles R. Humphrey, became part of the all-white hospital staff. The mayor promised us that no poor, rural, weak, or black person would ever have to bear the additional burden of being deprived of the opportunity for an education, a job, or simple justice. We didn't walk down the streets holding hands with the white people singing "We Shall Overcome," but as the mayor began to deliver on his promises of new industry and greater government financial support, the white people who chose to remain in the town subtly shifted from open hostility to some level of tolerance.

I didn't know until much later that Mayor Evers was constantly harassed by the KKK. "Some people can go to bed with a good book," he said. "I'd go to bed with a good threat and a shotgun under my bed. I'd get these characters callin' all times of the day and night."

My father and his buddy Mr. Vest were so impressed with Mayor Evers that they both served as bodyguards for a period of time, without pay, just so they could be near a man of such obvious inner power and strength.

In the fall of 1970, the all-white Jefferson County School Board tried to come up with a plan to comply with the court's decision on integration. Their plan failed, because all but about a dozen white students left the Fayette public school system, some never to return, and others transferred to private academies. The white parents would not allow their children to be forced to go to school with black children. So many families just simply up and moved away. The ones that didn't move, who could not afford to move and could not afford to put their children in private schools, stayed but kept their children at home. The year after I graduated, there were no white students in our school at all.

Mayor Evers's efforts were not confined to Jefferson County, but infiltrated through surrounding counties as well. His influence was spread throughout Claiborne to the north, Wilkinson and Adams counties to the south. Mayor Evers's personality and charm were open to everyone he encountered, and he wanted to spread the spirit of cooperation and friendliness between blacks and whites all over. If he was walking down the streets, any citizen of our town could walk up to him and strike up a friendly conversation. He always had a quick handshake and a warm smile for all who met him, moving swiftly and surely with no hint of hesitation about him.

The black political groups that were talked about in the news media and on television didn't come into our town, and if they had, the mayor would have thrown them out. The Black Panther Party, the Alabama political group that was organized by the Student Nonviolent Coordinating Committee (SNCC), drew his sharpest attention. He did not allow members of this group to agitate the people in his town. He insisted that a panther was a violent animal, one that destroys, and he couldn't and wouldn't allow the town he was so carefully building to be destroyed by anyone.

The mayor also had little patience for the Mississippi

Freedom Democratic Party (MFDP), led by Aaron Henry, an almost entirely black group that was created in 1964 to challenge the legitimacy of the then white-only Mississippi Democratic Party. The local NAACP clearly agreed with the mayor's point of view, and so did the townspeople. He simply believed in unity for all. He said the MFDP was full of racists and camera seekers. It had tough organizers, but they weren't exactly hoping to work alongside or with the whites. This didn't sit well with Mayor Evers.

Nor did the fact that the federal government low-income housing units were only available to whites, despite the federal funding which was used to build them. Mayor Evers made them open to anyone meeting the necessary requirements. Lee and I filled out an application and got accepted. The government housing was located less than three-quarters of a mile outside of the center of town on Highway 61 North.

We promptly moved into a three-bedroom, one-bath brick house with central heating. This was, by far, the best house Lee and I had lived in since being married. Our rent was forty dollars a month. Government housing rent is usually based on one's income. We had been living in our new house about a year and a half before Lee lost the job he had finally gotten with the power plant. He had to go back to odd jobs here and there, and we went back to just barely getting by, scraping just enough sometimes to pay the rent.

Almost two years after Nikki was born we had our second child. We named her Teresa LaShea. I loved both my babies, but I knew I didn't want any more children. Those two pregnancies certainly fulfilled my need to be a mother.

Lee was steadily getting worse—so obsessively and insanely jealous that I became a prisoner in my own home. Lee would fly into a jealous rage if I was caught talking to a man, *any* man, other than a well-known relative. He was constantly accusing me of doing him wrong in some way or another, probably because he knew in his own heart that he was the one doing wrong.

I have since learned that such outlandish jealousy is not born of love; it's born of insecurity within oneself. One by one, those rages became like nails in my coffin, locking me into an eternity of death. I felt as if I was suffocating and desperately gasping for breath.

Lee's drinking on weekends soon turned into a daily habit. His alcohol of choice was vodka on the weekends and beer during the week. I had heard rumors back in high school that he was known for not being able to hold his liquor, so his drinking escalated to the point of him becoming a borderline sloppy drunk. He'd leave home on Friday nights and would not come back until Sunday nights, using his earnings from odd jobs to party and drink. Rumors had also been flying around about him having affairs, and finally one day I mustered up the courage to ask him about one I'd heard about more than once.

"Yes," he said. "Now what are you going to do about it?" and he spat in my face.

His breath reeked of alcohol. He told me that the woman in question was also having his baby. I didn't believe him, thinking that was just one more tactic he was using to try and hurt me. It would be five years before I found out that he was telling the truth.

Nikki, being the first grandchild in Lee's family, was the apple of everyone's eye.

Both my babies were perfect as far as I was concerned. I could see right away the differences between their little personalities. Shea was an easier baby to care for. She wasn't as outgoing and didn't demand as much attention as her sister.

She was more an introvert, while Nikki kept me on my toes, never wanting to take a nap or have quiet time. She was tiny but had the personality of a giant.

Right after Shea was born Lee tried to persuade me to think about having yet another child. He said he wanted us to keep trying until we had a boy. I was young and naive, but I wasn't stupid. I knew we could have a house full of children and still have neither a boy nor a good marriage. Our marriage, I sensed, was at a point of no return for many reasons: Lee's inability to keep a steady job, his drinking, his affairs, but mostly because we both knew we didn't love each other enough to keep up the charade. I needed to take some steps to prepare for the separation I felt was inevitable.

I secretly went to the free local health department in town to get started taking birth control pills. I knew that if Lee ever found out he would have destroyed them. I kept that my little secret. I also took a night class, a year-long course in typing and shorthand class that prepared me for secretarial work. If a secretary job became available nearby, I now knew I had the qualifications to apply for it.

After serving as mayor for a year and half, Evers grew restless, and in 1971, he decided to run for governor. He was the first black man to ever attempt to become governor of Mississippi—not New York, Illinois, or California, but the old Magnolia State itself, the very bastion of the Deep South.

He knew he had gained the support of the people in Jefferson County. His name was known, and he had proven himself by keeping and making good on his word to the voters. But was that enough to get him elected governor? He wanted the people to know that if he was elected, he could do so much more, not only for Jefferson County, but for the whole state.

Mayor Evers had most, if not all, of the black support in the surrounding counties as well, but he knew that black votes alone would not be enough to get him elected; he needed statewide support. He had always talked big and had always supported the Democratic Party, but he decided to run as an Independent, saying that the party didn't matter as long as we had the right man in office. The focus should always be on the man not the party. He ran as an Independent so that he wouldn't have to participate in the Democratic Party–mandated primaries. That way he knew he would be running against only one candidate in November. Otherwise, he might have been eliminated before the November election.

His first promise as governor, if elected, was the same as most politicians, then and now: to cut taxes. If our taxes were cut each time a politician made that promise, we wouldn't be paying any taxes at all.

Life Magazine did an article on Evers running for governor. That article attracted a vast amount of out-of-state white liberals to come into Mississippi. They wanted to work in Evers's campaign. Mayor Evers's campaign headquarters was flooded with letters from both black and white young people from all over the United States, wanting to be a part of getting the first black man elected as governor in the Deep South.

Joe Rossignol was one of those white young liberals.

4
Joe Rossignol's Trip to Mississippi

In April 1971, Joe Rossignol stopped at the campus bookstore at the University of Santa Clara, where he was attending college. Browsing through the racks, he found a book that changed the course of his life. As he turned the book carousel around, his eyes focused on *Coming of Age in Mississippi* by Anne Moody. The book was about her experiences while growing up in rural Mississippi. The ending of the book was an account of a carload of people who were going to Washington to march in 1963.

After devouring the book in just two days, Joe was deeply disturbed by what he had read. The very next month, around May 14, Joe saw an article in *Life Magazine* about Charles Evers, the first black man to run for governor of Mississippi. The dangers Evers was facing as a candidate were illustrated with a picture of him, sitting at his kitchen table with a sawed-off shotgun across his lap. The caption under Evers's picture states, "Concerned over his personal safety, Evers keeps a modified carbine in his Fayette apartment for protection."

Members of the KKK, Kluxers as they were called, continually harassed him, calling all hours of the day and night, threatening death if he didn't back off. Anonymous threatening letters also made their way to Evers's headquarters.

This picture made a lasting impression on Joe. After reading the article, he was convinced that he wanted to be a part of Evers's history-making political campaign. He sat down

Figure 4. Father William J. Morrissey

and wrote the Evers campaign headquarters a letter, asking about coming to Mississippi to work with the voter registration. He waited anxiously for a reply. A few weeks later, he received a letter from an Evers representative, explaining what would be expected of him if he chose to work as a volunteer. The letter added at the end, "Yes, come on down," reminding Joe that his duties would be strictly on a volunteer basis. The Evers campaign office would provide him with room and board but no pay. This did not deter Joe. He packed his belongings and headed to Mississippi without telling his parents.

Evers felt that the best way to get more blacks registered statewide, and to give more blacks the courage to run for office in other rural counties, was for him to run for governor. He wanted other blacks to know that if you are qualified, you have the right to run for any office of your choosing. He also knew that the resistance against his becoming mayor of a small, predominantly black town like Fayette, Mississippi, was small potatoes compared to the resistance he would face in seeking the office of governor of Mississippi. Even with a massive successful voter registration drive, only 30 percent of the registered voters in Mississippi were black, and getting white votes would be a major challenge. Thus, Evers (off the record) knew he couldn't possibly win if efforts weren't multiplied tenfold to encourage more and more blacks to register. In order to do this, he knew he needed to accept the help of volunteers, both black and white, from all over the country, volunteers who also believed in "equal rights for all." Whereas registering black voters for the mayoral election was mainly done by black people, now both blacks and whites would be working together, although the major portion of the white volunteers did not grow up in the South.

Evers's goals were to encourage more blacks to register, run a positive campaign for himself, and to *be alive* on election day, November 2, 1971, to witness it all. These goals met Joe's expectations, which made him eager to join Evers's campaign staff.

During that summer, we had hundreds of young men and women, mostly white, coming to our state to live and work with black families. Many local residents called the newcomers *invaders, communist agents,* and *do-gooders.* Even some members of the black community did not trust those young people, believing that they came south to challenge the laws, but felt that when things got rough, they would up and leave for some other lark. In reality, those young people were just middle- and upper-class young Americans, willing to risk their lives for a worthy cause.

Some southerners (both black and white) believed that the outsiders coming into Mississippi would have a negative effect on the residents of Jefferson County, and that could create a great amount of resentment which could only be released by violence. Some believed these young people were sent to save the black man's body and the white man's soul. They forgot that the purpose of the community was to help those young volunteers work in developing the entire community's strength, for both blacks and whites.

Joe's family was from up north, in New York City, where he spent the first seven years of his life. His family then moved to Brookfield Center and then New Milford, Connecticut. His parents had five children, three boys and two girls, and Joe was the second child. He was a very strong and levelheaded guy, traits that enabled him to withstand the pressures unleashed upon him when he was registering voters.

He arrived in Fayette on his twenty-second birthday, June 7, 1971, and had just finished college but skipped out on his graduation because the main speaker was John Wayne. Having marched in many anti–Vietnam/Cambodia protests in San Francisco, he wasn't about to stay and listen to John Wayne's hawkish right-winged opinions.

From the Volunteers into Mississippi Fact Sheet he'd received from Father William J. Morrissey, SSJ, a white priest and activist working with the Evers campaign, Joe knew that volunteers would not have a leadership role, but would follow instructions of the local black political leaders (and like-minded whites). Local residents, who provided lodging and food, might not have indoor plumbing or even an extra bed for a volunteer. Those volunteers were advised to bring sleeping bags, a washcloth, soap, Band-Aids, aspirin, whatever prescribed medication they might be currently taking, sensible shoes (walking would be a necessity), loose-fitting clothing to accommodate the extreme humidity and heat (nothing flashy, but conservative), and an open-mindedness about working through church leadership. Political activity in Mississippi was conducted along with preaching, hymn singing, and working with the Lord's assistance. Workdays would often run from very early in the morning until well into the night.

Would-be volunteers who in any way, shape, or form wanted to subvert the black effort were strongly encouraged to stay home. If anyone was thinking about establishing some kind of southern political power base of his own, coming to Mississippi was definitely not going to be a good experience. Women volunteers were even warned that southerners would not take kindly to them if they constantly wore blue jeans; for women to wear any kind of pants was not acceptable in our area of the South at that time.

Armed with his Volunteers into Mississippi Fact Sheet and his determination to participate in this cause, Joe made his entrance into Mississippi, driving a white 1967 Austin-Healey Sprite with a chrome roll bar. (Volunteers were encouraged to bring their own transportation.) His long, flaming-red hair was blowing in the wind. (Apparently he'd overlooked the point on the fact sheet about "long hair needs to be cut to a reasonable length," but to be quite honest, he probably didn't even give it a second thought. This is a man who would and, to this day, still does open a can of tuna, add mayonnaise to the can, stir it a little, and eat it directly from the can—not exactly a candidate for the GQ magazine.)

To make matters worse, his California license plate earmarked him as the young Democrat liberal that he was. ("We ask individuals to avoid extremes in dress and/or appearance that would only serve to reinforce the fact that you are an 'outsider' and represent a lifestyle very foreign to the area to which you may be assigned.") No one had noticed his hair when he campaigned for the original antiwar candidate, Eugene McCarthy, in the 1968 primary in Omaha, Nebraska.

Right from the start, Joe's mere presence antagonized some of the local rednecks. He started working in a region that was considered the most dangerous part of the state, seething with hatred, and with few restraints against white violence that was unleashed upon anyone trying to help the blacks. Soon after arriving, he clearly understood that he had his work cut out for him. Reading about the southern black experience was a whole lot different from actually living in it.

His assignment was to spend weeks stirring up dust on the back roads of rural southwest Mississippi as he attempted to register local *colored* people to vote. His personal contact was Father Morrissey, and since the priest was from Cedarhurst, Long Island, and Joe from New York City, the two immediately hit it off. Father Morrissey took his new volunteer to Lum's, a local eatery in Natchez, for a get-acquainted lunch, which to Joe's surprise included several beers. Beer at lunch with a Catholic priest initiated for him what would turn out to be a highly unusual summer experience.

During lunch, Father, as he was later called by all who knew him, gave Joe his first assignment. He verbally gave him directions on how to get to Gloster, a small community in Amite County, seven miles from the Louisiana border and not far north of Baton Rouge. To someone who had never been to Gloster, the directions sounded very vague. "Go fifteen miles south on Liberty Road, take a right on Highway 33, cross three bridges, and take a right at the blue mailbox. Then go one mile and look for Maggie Hunt's house on the left." The Hunt family would provide him room and board. They, too, were big supporters of Charles Evers.

To Joe's amazement, Father told him to immediately phone in after he arrived at the Hunts' house to let him know that he had not run into any incidents along the way. "Registering voters in the South can be dangerous work if one isn't careful." Joe was warned numerous times about the dangers of Mississippi: take precautions, beware of cars without tags, never go out alone, always watch for cops without badges, and never go out after dark. Going out alone was against the most fundamental rules of the voter registration. It was too easy for something to happen to a volunteer if there weren't any witnesses around.

Law enforcement varied from county to county. County sheriffs and other local officials, whose power would be hard for a northern city dweller to imagine, ranged from peaceful to vicious. The volunteers had learned all too well that the definition of violence depended on *who* was committing the violence and *how* a society could conspire *with* or *against* them. With virtually no local protection, especially in some of the rural counties, fear became the ever-present climate of life.

The volunteers also quickly learned what to expect from the Mississippi policemen: harassment, arrest, and jail. Never before had they been exposed to the grinding poverty, official lawlessness, and demeaning caste restrictions that were the daily bread for the black population.

With Father's vague directions, Joe found the Hunts' house. He also discovered that most of the directions given to other places would be very similar as Father Morrissey became instrumental in sending Joe on his journey throughout the summer.

During Joe's four years of college at Santa Clara University, his Catholic religion had taken a backseat. Even though he was attending a Catholic Jesuit school, he never attended Mass or any religious events. After years of catechism, Catholic Youth Organization, and going to Mass every Sunday, he couldn't wait to give up those activities. In fact, years later while visiting his mother at her home in Connecticut, he noticed she didn't attend church on Sundays anymore, either. When asked, his mother noted that she only went for her children's sake, and she had stopped going when they all left home.

Assigned to work with Father Morrissey, Joe reconnected himself once again with the Catholic Church. Each Sunday Joe attended Mass in Fayette. Afterward, Father met with the parishioners to mingle and talk for a few minutes. There was one lady in particular who stuck out because she always wore big fancy hats. That was my sister Dot. Father never failed to observe and make a positive comment about her hats, but Joe only knew her as Mrs. Robinson and never really talked with her, though he never forgot her either.

When Joe began his work in Gloster, it only took a few days for all the locals to know they had a stranger in town. He quickly found himself attached to one community. The local rednecks wanted no part of him and made every attempt to alienate him, but the blacks bent over backward to make him feel right at home.

Gloster was like many a southern town. The Georgia-Pacific lumber mill was the main employer. The railroad was the primary method of shipping its products. The train tracks divided the town whites on one side, blacks on the other. The police station was in the middle of the two but positioned on the white side of the tracks. It was very important to know which side was the right side.

Since Charles Evers was running for governor against William "Bill" Waller, a white Democrat, it was necessary to acquire as many registered blacks as possible, hoping they would exercise their rights on voting day. Blacks in 1965, thanks to Lyndon B. Johnson's Civil Rights Voter Registration Act, had gained the right of voting, but many remained unregistered due to fear and intimidation on the part of southern whites. Blacks had to be educated about what the right to vote was all about. Even though Mayor Evers, with the help of his fellow workers, volunteers, and friends, had managed to register enough black voters for the mayoral election of 1969, more blacks had turned eighteen (the now legal age to vote, which created even a wider base for potential votes), and they needed to be registered; some had never bothered, and many elderly blacks remained uneducated in the process, refusing to take part. Voting potential of over half the black population of Mississippi remained untapped. Even some blacks in Fayette thought they had already done their part by voting in the mayoral election and didn't understand why they needed to vote again. "We did our part, now they's askin' us to do it again." Unregistered blacks in other Mississippi counties were even harder to persuade.

People who had registered in the past had to reregister at the circuit clerk's office in the appropriate courthouse, because some of the supervisory boundaries had been changed. If the person's name wasn't in the right book, at the right courthouse, he lost his voting rights. Those living in cities or towns also had to register in the city clerk's office in order to vote for officials in town or city elections.

Imagine if you've never been educated, never known the power of the vote, never understood that anything could change; why would you go to the trouble of doing something you were afraid of, something you thought was going to take even more money out of your meager-to-nonexistent finances, something for which you thought you might be killed by the whites if you tried to do it? And, if you had gathered the courage to vote once, wasn't that enough?

Fear was the operative word for Joe while every day he tried his best to convince potential black voters of the necessity to exercise their rights. Though many blacks' protests that they could neither read nor write, Joe and the other volunteers patiently explained that only their mark was required to have their names written in the proper book.

The more involved he became with voter registration, the more he realized his life was at risk. Some of the towns he worked in, such as Liberty, had an exceptionally long history of racial violence. As volunteers doggedly trudged onward, door to door, white agitators' tempers flared even higher. "Save the South" attitudes fanned the flames of hatred into burning rage.

In hot, humid, almost unbearable weather, Joe spent much of the summer driving along the dusty back roads in search of potential voters. Many of the roads were dirt mixed with gravel. God help it if it hadn't rained for days on end. The county was dry as a bone. During dry spells, a vehicle could pass by and leave a cloud of dust so thick that it took several minutes to settle, and if a car was coming behind, it had to almost come to a crawl in order to see the road.

Joe and the other volunteers learned quickly to use county maps to help them with directions. The biggest problem they encountered was not being able to tell a poor black shack from a poor white shack. The poverty and the misery of the neighborhoods were evident. No one could deny the existence of oppression in the North, but it was much stronger and more oppressive in Mississippi and throughout the South.

The young volunteers worked from sunup to sundown. Sometimes the humidity was so high that their clothing was soaking wet after only a few minutes of work. Still, they kept going from door to door. Whenever they knocked on a door and a white person answered it, they would still politely ask if household members were registered voters or not. Many of the poor whites were nice enough, but others were hostile because they knew about those volunteers and why they were there.

In some of the small southern towns, Joe came to believe the local whites were particularly proud and edgy, but he also believed that it was the pride of poor, uneducated people still living in the past. For some of those people, life was an ongoing ordeal of poverty, superstition, and ignorance, which were overwhelming.

Having grown up in an upper-middle-class family, Joe was truly appalled by the poverty he saw everywhere. In some ways, he even understood why the average, poor ignorant whites attempted to oppress the local poor, uneducated blacks. There was only so much pie to be divided up; why should they want others to be able to get more? During his stay, he saw cardboard covering holes in floors and newspapers being used for wallpaper in both black and white homes. He saw children barely clothed or bathed, eating out of tin dishes, sitting on the porch, desolate, despondent, no light in their eyes.

Those volunteers considered acquiring three new registered black voters per day a victory because the local white establishment was so proficient at discouraging black registration. One of the difficulties was that most blacks were instinctively and extremely apprehensive of the word *registration*. They connected it with going to the courthouse and answering a lengthy, trickily worded form. Also, some thought they would have to pay a fee to register, associating it with the poll tax, which was still a requirement in state elections.

Whenever the volunteers found someone who agreed to register, they had to be sure to be at that residence early the next morning to take that person to the courthouse before the individual changed his or her mind. Sometimes, they were able to encourage whole families to go. The process usually took all day because the county clerk would stall to make them squirm, and oftentimes, the procedure was so intimidating that many potential voters just refused to register. Usually, by late afternoon, well after lunch, the clerk finally abided by his federally mandated rules and let the people register. The volunteers were always on hand to help them even through the sitting and waiting, especially the ones who could not read or write. If registration was denied for some reason or another, or discouraged in any way, by anyone at the courthouse, the volunteers had to try to convince the people to appeal according to their constitutional rights or file affidavits with the Elections Commission. This was not an easy task.

While the volunteers were working the rural towns in Mississippi, the KKK made its presence known even more. Joe learned that they had been watching and monitoring his every move. He and another volunteer were working their way down a rural road that eventually led to a small town called Smithdale. At the end of the day, on their drive back to their temporary home in Gloster, they noticed nothing unusual about the blacktop road they were on.

The next morning, that same road had three big letters painted in white across the pavement: KKK. Joe had his fellow worker take a picture of him and his car in front of the letters as a reminder of his voter registration days. Throughout all these years, Joe kept a copy he'd found of the Application for Citizenship in the Invisible Empire, United Klans of America, Inc., Knights of the Ku Klux Klan:

I, the undersigned, a native born, true and loyal citizen of the United States of America, being a white male

Gentile person of temperate habits, sound in mind, and a believer in the tenets of the Christian religion, the maintenance of White Supremacy and the Principles of a "pure Americanism," do most respectively apply for membership in the United Klans of America, Knights of the Ku Klux Klan through Klan No._____, Realm of_____.

I guarantee on my honor to conform strictly to all rules and requirements regulating my "naturaliza-tion" and the continuance of my membership, and at all times a strict and loyal obedience to your constitu-tional authority and the constitution and laws of the fraternity, not in conflict with the constitution and constitutional laws of the United States of America and the states thereof. If I prove untrue as a Klansman I will willingly accept as my portion whatever penalty your authority may impose.

The required "klectokon" accompanies this application. (Webster's dictionary gives no definition of a klectokon.) The application has two signature lines for Klansmen securing the application and a signature line for the applicant, with two lines underneath that signature for both residence and business addresses. Along the bottom is stated, "If You Are For A Purely White America If You Are Against Commu-nist-Inspired Race Mixing If You Are A True Patriot JOIN TODAY!"

The following week, the KKK burned a cross on the Hunts' lawn, the house where Joe was staying. Once a cross was burned, that unpleasant incident was supposed to put enough fear into a family that they would move away. It worked with some, but not all, and it didn't work with the Hunt family. The Klan thought that the more people they could frighten and intimidate into moving away, the less votes Charles Evers would receive. Charles Evers was the KKK's "public enemy number one," as stated in a reprinted copy of a *Playboy* interview with Evers, October 1971.

Socially intermingling with blacks was an eye-opening experience for Joe. He learned that something so simple as buying gas for his car could be a supreme hassle. None of the white-owned gas stations would serve him, and he had to plan his route to include a black-owned Texaco station whenever he needed gasoline.

At no time was Joe treated badly by his local hosts. They appreciated him and all that he was trying to do. He was always invited to attend NAACP meetings or any other functions that were held by blacks. People showed up in force to support the local NAACP meetings and made everyone feel welcome by singing "We Shall Overcome" while holding hands.

One of the pleasures of Joe's tenure in Mississippi was being able to visit the area where Anne Moody grew up. Although he did not meet her (since she had already left Mississippi by that time), he was able to visit with many people who did know her and to visit her home site.

After weeks of campaigning in Amite County, Joe was told to report back to Father Morrissey in Natchez, and over the next few weeks, he found various ways to help Father. As the volunteer workers with the longer tenure slowly left to return home, he swiftly rose to the top and found himself the long-termer. (Volunteers were asked to work three- or four-week blocks of time.) He became Father's driver and chief gofer and also became an important figure in the Natchez headquarters. This led to a good working relationship with Father until the priest's death in 1985. During the week, Joe spent long hours working the streets of the black neighborhoods, helping people complete voter registrations and setting up the Evers for Governor campaign office in Natchez. Natchez lies along the Mississippi River. It's a beautiful city with numerous grand old plantations, full of old southern charm. It was quite a change from the back roads of Gloster, Liberty, Centreville, and other surrounding towns that Joe had previously worked.

This was a very exciting and educational time for Joe. He met and worked with some of the great black leaders of Mississippi, such as Charles Evers, Aaron Henry, Fannie Lou Hamer, Henry Kirksey, and Barney Schoby, a black civil rights activist who would later file a class-action lawsuit attacking a county-wide redistricting plan adopted by and for the election of the Adams County Board of Supervisors. He also met such national figures as Coretta Scott King, Julian Bond, John Lewis, New York mayor John Lindsay, and Allard Lowenstein, who was a leader in the ongoing civil rights and antiwar movements. By the end of the campaign, Joe knew as much about Mississippi as most native-born residents.

The election was held on November 2, 1971. Charles Evers lost the election, but he won the battle. Although his white opponent won, Evers still paved the way for many blacks across the state to seek and gain political offices, and Evers became our greatest hope. The image of a black hand and a white hand clasped together, which originated with the Student Nonviolent Coordinating Committee (SNCC), became the symbol of that Evers campaign and to this day, Joe is very proud of the fact that he helped to paint the large mural of those hands over Evers's campaign headquarters.

Back in high school when I wore that pin with the black and white hands clasped together fastened to my shirt while entering Porter's Café, I never dreamed I'd someday meet someone who had a hand in painting that very symbol on the wall of Mayor Evers's campaign headquarters located on Franklin Street in Natchez.

When the election was over, Joe went to work for Aaron Henry, who was the chairman of the state Democratic Party. After working with him for a few months, Joe returned to California. Upon his return to the corporate culture of Hewlett-Packard, he found he missed the commitment he'd had in Mississippi and missed the openness and the acceptance the people offered him as a person. He also missed the life he'd had there, which was always full of surprises, some not so good, but forever exciting.

A year and a half passed before he finally decided that he wanted to go back to the South and start a new life. A few days later, he was on Amtrak, headed for New Orleans, where Father Morrissey was waiting at the train station to pick him up. The long drive back to Natchez gave them a chance to catch up on all the things that had happened during his absence. Joe asked about the job market, and Father told him about the supermarket that was opening up that same week in Fayette.

Charles Evers had negotiated with Rayvon Smith, a white businessman from Jackson, to build a minimall in Fayette. By then, Evers had been mayor for over two years. Joe was interviewed on his second day in town and hired as an assistant manager.

5
The Deterioration of Marriage

As time went on, Lee's and my marriage increasingly deteriorated. We argued about anything and everything to the point that Lee started to push me around, getting up close in my face. He'd hiss ugly words at me, his face no more than a hairsbreadth away.

I didn't want my daughters to be raised in that environment. After four years of marriage to Lee and much consideration, I knew I had come to the end of my rope; I decided it was time to get out. There had to a better life for my children and me. To be strong and strike out on my own was the driving force within me. I needed a plan, and the first step would be to leave Lee. Divorce could come later. Leaving with two little children, Nikki, four, Shea, two years and ten months, would not be easy, but I had to manage somehow. The fire that burned deep inside of me made me want more than to simply *exist*; I wanted to *live*.

Timing was of utmost importance, because if I didn't pick the right moment, things could quickly accelerate out of control. Lee was not the type of man to sit back and allow me to walk out of his life peacefully; he had his pride to protect. I had to be very careful not to make matters any worse.

How was I going to leave him without a fight, and where would I go when I did? The answer came one cold, early November night in 1973. As I lay in bed with our two children, Lee came home intoxicated and placed the tip of a gun barrel up against my left temple. Even before I felt the cold steel, I smelled the strong scent of alcohol on his breath as he spewed out obscenities.

Afraid to open my eyes or move a muscle, I pretended to be sleeping. He kept nudging my temple with the gun barrel, while ordering me to wake up. I *still* did not move. My body was gripped with fear as I lay there, wondering how I was going to escape this nightmare. After a few minutes, which seemed more like hours, Lee collapsed onto the floor next to the bed in a drunken stupor.

That was my opportunity to get out of the house. I leaped from the bed, leaving the children asleep, and ran next door to a neighbor's house to call the police. When the police arrived, Lee was still passed out cold with the gun lying beside him.

He was carted off to jail, and the very next day I left. I knew I had to act quickly. He wouldn't be in jail for long because I had refused to press charges against him. I just wanted him out of the house. I was told by the police that if I didn't press charges, they could only hold him overnight or until he sobered up. All of this happened on a Friday night, so I knew he'd be there until Monday. That would give me enough time to get away. I packed what little we had, took the children, and went back to live with my father and Louberta again. By then they had moved back together and built a Federal Housing Administration (FHA) house off Highway 553 west about three miles outside of Fayette. The aunt and uncle had since deceased.

When Lee got out of jail, he got a job with Fayette Enterprises, a lumber company located on Highway 33. As soon as he started working, he came to me, wanting us to get back together and apply to have an FHA house built. I refused both offers. How could we make a mortgage payment when we couldn't pay rent without the help of our families? Who knew how long that job was going to last with his work habits? Besides, I knew my life with him was over.

The first thing I needed to do after my separation from Lee was to try and get a job. I tried to find a secretary job, but none was available at the time. I had heard cashiers were needed at the new supermarket in town. I went there and applied and was told to come in the following day. I went to work at New Deal Supermarket in November 1973, a week before Thanksgiving. Joe Rossignol was the assistant manager. The manager, Larry Smith, nephew of Rayvon Smith, the owner, said they needed full-time cashiers as business was booming.

Being employed was an important step in the right direction if I was to make a life on my own. This job would provide income for my children and me while I got our lives sorted out. This was the first job I'd ever had in my entire life. Something about working towards a goal gave me a certain amount of pride, and just knowing that I could take care of my children financially was certainly going to be a relief.

My first week was supposed to have been spent in training, as I had never used a cash register before. Thank goodness I caught on quickly, because before the week was out I was running the register all by myself with hardly any mistakes, and with pride, I might add. The store was very busy, which made the first week go by in a whirlwind.

The second week on the job I saw a red-haired young man come swinging through the glass sliding doors of the store. My first thought when I saw him was "Why in the world did he dye his hair that color?" It was *flaming* red. I said to myself, "He must be one of those young white liberals I heard about who came into our town to help with voter registration." I could tell from his accent that he wasn't from Mississippi. Besides, he just didn't have that southern look about him.

His hair was touching his shoulders, and he was wearing little gold wire-rimmed glasses. His appearance reminded me of those hippies I had seen on television. He wore some brown and white oxfords, which were not popular at all in our town. I did notice, in time, he must have had two pairs of those shoes because he sometimes wore blue and white ones as well.

During the course of the day, I noticed other employees talking to him. Everyone seemed to know him except me. By the third day I was there, I looked up and saw him approaching me. As he neared, I quickly turned my head, which made him pass on by. He seemed to be at ease with the other employees but his friendliness made me very uneasy. Each time I saw him coming toward me, I turned my head, pretending I was too busy to notice him. My experiences talking to any white person were very limited. I think the longest conversation I'd ever had with a white person was back in my senior year in high school in Mr. Gavin's office when he had asked me to explain the clash between Marilyn Nations and me. I never had any kind of conversation with the white students that I had attended school with, and I definitely didn't have any experience talking one-on-one with a young white man.

It probably would have been a wise idea to have asked someone who he was, but my mind just wasn't focused on him. It was always so hectic in the store; I hardly had time to think. This job also gave me an opportunity to see people that I wouldn't have otherwise seen on a daily basis, which kept me focused as well. It really felt good to be out talking with people, even if it was during working hours. Being friendly with the customers was part of the job, however short the conversations were, and was a part I thoroughly enjoyed.

I continued to keep my distance from that strange-looking young white man because I didn't know what I would say if he tried to initiate a conversation with me. He noticed my indifference and finally left me alone—for a while, anyway.

Two weeks passed, and I was still ignoring him, but I did learn his name was Joe and, like me, he was a new employee at the supermarket. I didn't know what his job title was or why it seemed so necessary for him to introduce himself to me. No one thought it was important enough to inform me that he was the assistant manager, which made him my boss. I was too busy trying to get used to my new job and comprehend all that was going on, in and around town. Everything that was happening was so new and exciting. Furthermore, ever present on my mind was the fact that I still had my dead marriage to deal with. I had not seen or heard from Lee since I had refused his offer of getting back together and applying for a house, and that wasn't necessarily a good thing.

The new grocery store was always crowded with busy shoppers and browsers. All of our customers so far were black, and they seemed happy just to have a store they could come in, browse and shop at their leisure, and not have to wait at the end of a line to be waited on. The atmosphere was especially relaxed and pleasant.

The white people stayed away initially, but once they did decide to come in and shop, they went to Mr. Smith and asked him if he would consider hiring white checkers to wait on them. They actually wanted him to hire white checkers to wait on the white customers and black checkers for the black customers. He told them he would never consider that. Business went on as usual, and the few whites who remained in town started reluctantly coming in to shop.

The new mall, in which the supermarket was housed, also had a brand-new liquor store, a dollar store, and the Fayette Bank. The liquor store was also owned by Rayvon Smith. Before then, we had only one bank (Jefferson County Bank) in town, and it was owned by a local white family, the Trulys. The Jefferson County Bank had been around as long as I could remember, and it was never a friendly bank for blacks. That was the same bank from which, years back, my father had borrowed to buy his first tractor. I had never been in that bank, but I know the only black people one would see there were customers, standing and waiting for their turns, and the people who cleaned it.

At the new bank, I finally saw black tellers working behind the windows for the first time. Customers could actually walk in and be greeted by a smiling face, not stared at as if they didn't belong. It was a wonderful feeling to be able to complete a transaction in a pleasant atmosphere without feeling hurried or intimidated. It was amazing to see people leisurely standing around, swapping small talk as if they didn't have a care in the world. No more standing at the back of the line until all the white patrons had been waited on. It was such a captivating time in our town. Each day seemed to have brought about something new and exciting. There were so many things to look forward to besides meeting that new red-haired man in the store.

Joe still had been giving me those sly looks each time he passed my station. He had not tried to approach me again, but I caught him staring at me several times throughout the day. Without our ever having officially met, I felt this white man had an attraction for me, which made me feel weird and a little excited. It was almost frightening and certainly unthinkable. He seemed like a nice enough guy, but why in the world would he be interested in me, a black woman?

I suppose he got tired of me ignoring him and he finally walked up to me one day and introduced himself, saying, "Hi, my name is Joe."

I didn't know what to say or do. All I could come back with was, "So?" I felt really stupid, but it had popped out, and I couldn't take it back. He then went on to tell me that he was the assistant manager. As he was talking, I wanted to somehow disappear. I think if I had had an Adam's apple I would have swallowed it. The blood rushed to my head, which made me dizzy and barely able to stand. I quickly hid my sweaty palms behind my back, trying to hide my nervousness. Why on God's green earth hadn't someone found it necessary to tell me who this man was? He was *my boss*, for goodness sake. During that short conversation, I made up my mind what I had to do. My thoughts were buzzing around in my head. I don't think I heard anything else he said past that he was the assistant manager.

After that introduction, I knew I had to quit. I was sure when Larry found out how I had been treating Joe, he was going to fire me anyway. I also couldn't cope with the obvious interest of this white-faced, red-haired stranger who was my boss, no less. With my mind made up, I was thinking, *If only I could get through this day,* which seemed like it would never end. The hours on the clock slowly ticked by; my shift would not be over until 5:00 p.m., and it was only 11:00 a.m. I thought about going for lunch and not returning but decided against that idea. I knew the importance of finishing out my shift. That had to be one of the longest days of my life, and believe me, I've had a few in my time. I didn't know what excuse I would use to quit, but I had to find something.

I know it probably sounds dreadfully inane by today's standards, but I was terribly ashamed and afraid of having someone of a different race pay so much attention to me. Since Mr. Evers had come to town, jobs weren't that difficult to come by, and I felt I could easily find other employment and not have to deal with either Joe or the embarrassment of being fired.

The next morning, not knowing what to do, I did nothing, not even calling in to lie and say I was sick. I was sitting around nervously twiddling my thumbs when the phone rang about an hour after I should have been at work. Startled, I picked up the receiver and said, "Hello." The voice on the other end said, "Martha, this is Larry Smith. I'm calling to find out why you didn't come in this morning."

Stuttering, I said, "I didn't know Joe was the assistant manager."

He said, "Yes, so what?"

I was a little baffled by his attitude, but I said, "Well, he's been trying to introduce himself to me for a few days now and each time I ignored him."

After a short silence, he asked, "What's that got to do with you coming to work?"

"Well," I said, "I thought when he told you what I had done, you were going to fire me, so I decided to quit before I got fired."

He said, "Martha, come in because we need you very much. The shop is full, and there is no time to replace you on such short notice."

There were only four cash registers, and when it was that busy we usually had them all running. With that argument, I couldn't put up much of a fuss. I was the fourth checker. He said, "I'll send Joe to pick you up, and that will give you guys a chance to talk and clear the air between you."

I said thank you and hung up, happy that I hadn't lost my job but apprehensive about Joe picking me up. I hurriedly got dressed, put my coat on, and waited nervously by the front door, peeping out the window watching for the arrival of his car. My stomach was churning queasily. When he arrived, I dashed out the door, not giving him a chance to think about coming in. On the ride back, Joe and I did a lot of talking, and to my surprise, I found him to be smart, witty, and very secure about who he was. He told me he attended the Catholic church, St. Anne's, in town every Sunday with Father Morrissey. He talked about some of the families he'd met there—the Brinkleys, the Franklins, and the Collinses. Finally, he told me about this lady that came with two little girls who always wore these big unique hats. He said she wore the most fascinating hats he'd ever seen. Wow! I knew exactly who he was talking about because that lady was my sister Dot. He was very shocked to find out that the hat lady was related to me. That kind of broke the ice between us, and I guess it gave him the courage to ask, "Why do you always look so sad?"

I wasn't ready to talk about my failed marriage with *anyone*, and certainly not with a white stranger. I just looked away and kept silent, ignoring his question. We made a little small talk, and since we seemed to be a bit more at ease with each other, I took that opportunity to ask him a question that I had been curious about since the first time I had seen him. "Why did you dye your hair red?"

He smiled for a long time, moving his head slightly from side to side, with a rather astonished look on his face, acting like he was trying to suppress a hearty laugh. I guess he was trying to decide how to answer. Finally he said, matter-of-factly, "I didn't dye it. I was born a redhead."

My face flushed with embarrassment. Lordy, was I ever naïve! After that I kept my mouth closed for fear of saying something else stupid. I thought it best to just let him do the talking.

Joe didn't give up easily. He told me that I had beautiful

brown eyes but they held such a sad look in them. Barely being able to speak, I made up some lame excuse, hoping he'd stop prying into my personal life. Whatever I said, it was enough to stop him from asking any more questions for the remainder of the ride to work.

Once we got to work, there was no time to talk about anything, it was so busy. I quickly wrote in my time on the time card while rushing to get my register open to help take care of the long lines of customers. Under most circumstances, customers would have been irritable having to wait in line for such a long time, but these customers seemed to be enjoying themselves, talking with each other while waiting patiently.

Every time Joe walked by me that day, he always gave me a warm smile. I didn't know what to make of this man. He seemed nice enough and sincere, but he was *white*. A few days later, Joe walked up to me and asked me out to lunch. I immediately said, "No, I'm married."

His reply was, "I didn't ask you to marry me; I asked you to lunch."

I was taken aback. I thought that comment was very fresh of him. I didn't know how to respond to that. I was at a loss for words because he hadn't asked me to marry him; he had only asked me out to lunch. Hesitantly, I agreed to go with him. He suggested we have lunch at Evers Restaurant. Mayor Evers had been big on promoting black and white unity, and we knew we wouldn't be refused service there. On the way to the restaurant we hardly had any conversation. I was too shy to say much of anything. What little talking there was was done by Joe.

Sitting across the table from him, I felt embarrassed, ashamed, and scared. As we waited to be served a record came on the juke box—"Never Gonna Give You Up" by

Barry White. I was glad to hear a song I liked, which also gave me something to say. I blurted out, "Oh, I love that song by Isaac Hayes; it's one of my favorites."

He looked directly at me and said, "That's not Isaac Hayes; that's Barry White," and started to laugh.

That only embarrassed me more. Thank goodness I am dark skinned because had I been light skinned I would have turned the color of his hair. I must say, I did enjoy his lighthearted personality and his devilish conversation, but I couldn't help wondering what the people in the restaurant were thinking, seeing us together.

We were served lunch, but I could hardly eat, for I felt all eyes were upon us. I picked at my lunch, maybe eating only half, and I had to force that down. I did notice he cleaned his plate, no shame there. The hour passed swiftly, and it was time to go. I was glad to be out of there, even if it meant going back to work. When we got back, the other checkers were waiting, wanting to know how my lunch went. In between customers, my co-workers pressed me for every detail of my lunch with Joe. Thank goodness the store always stayed busy, leaving little time for conversation.

The rest of the day went by in a blur. It was hard to keep my mind from wandering. I repeatedly replayed that lunch date in my mind a thousand times. Every time I thought about it, a smile crept onto my face no matter how hard I tried to conceal it. The other girls at work quickly noticed my lack of interest and started teasing me. I shrugged their comments off like having lunch with one of the bosses was no big deal. I still wondered, why me?

Getting involved in a relationship with a man, any man, was the farthest thing from my mind. Each day, though, Joe found a few moments to spend with me. He always had something encouraging and sincere to say to me. He said I had the cutest smile if only I would show it more often. I couldn't imagine what he thought I had to smile about. Soon I began to look forward to his mini-visits, for they became the highlights of my day. I loved going to work. It was exciting, and each day held something even more special to look forward to. I wished I could have dressed a little nicer, but my wardrobe was very limited. I did the best I could with what I had, taking a little extra time each morning making sure my hair was well groomed and cared for.

I tried, at first, to resist the strong attraction between us, but after much pursuing from Joe, I finally gave in. Our relationship grew very intense from a very humble beginning. We literally fell in love while working in the store without having spent any quality time together. It was the looks, the mini-chats, and the warm words of encouragement he'd give me each day that broke down my defenses and made my heart flutter every time I saw him coming. The growth of our relationship was clearly expressed. I had to admit to myself that I had fallen in love with that fresh, young, redheaded, white liberal. Love does have a way of breaking through all barriers.

We didn't see each other very much at first, mostly confining our relationship to telephone conversations and an abundance of letter writing. Joe's handwriting was terrible. I'd spend days reading one letter over and over until I could finally figure out what he had written.

I looked forward to his letters. I cherished every one of them, hiding them under my mattress, for they were what helped me get through some of the difficult times during my separation from Lee and later the divorce. Those letters were such a source of strength. I'd reread them whenever I felt discouraged or depressed about the state my life was in. At the end of each letter, Joe always stressed that he would be waiting for me no matter how long it took.

When we finally started to spend time together in public, people started to gossip. Being the only black woman in town who was publicly dating a white man caused quite a stir. We were far too noticeable. Some reacted to our relationship with open hostility; some just stared boldly; still others merely whispered and shook their heads while walking by. I had to get used to the constant stares and whispers as part of the price I had to pay for dating someone outside of my race. Some of the whispering was probably caused by the fact that I was still legally a married woman, although I was no longer living with Lee. In no time at all, Joe and I became the talk of the town. People treated me as if I was contaminated, and whatever I had, no one wanted to catch it.

My father was more understanding, but that took a while. In light of all the talk that was going around, I had to tell my dad that I was seeing Joe. He wasn't happy about it at first. I think he worried that since Joe was a manager at the place I worked, I might have been coerced by him into a relationship. Each time Joe came to pick me up, however, he and my father made small talk, and gradually Daddy realized this was a relationship I very much wanted, and he became a little more cordial, finally getting comfortable enough to ask Joe to bring him a pack of Viceroy cigarettes when he knew he was coming by to pick me up.

I had been working at New Deal for about four months before I decided it was time to quit. By then Lee knew I was working there, and he had heard rumors of my and Joe's relationship. He'd show up unexpectedly and start asking me questions and harassing me in front of the customers. The straw that broke the camel's back was the day he came in, walked up to me while I was waiting on a customer, and snatched the food stamps that she had given me out of my hand and asked, "What the hell is going on between you and that white man?"

I was shocked and mortified by this unpleasant confrontation. I had to stop what I was doing and usher him out of the store, but not before Larry noticed what had happened. He told me that type of behavior was not good for business, and I had to do something to keep him away, or he'd be forced to get a restraining order against him. I knew Lee well enough to know that he wouldn't stay away just because I said so. His behavior prompted me to quit the first job I'd ever had and had become so fond of.

I also found I wasn't prepared for, nor could I get used to, the stares, the whispers, and the gossip I had begun to face every day. I knew what happened between Lee and me would only make things worse.

Lee came to my father's house to see the children and me, probably more likely to harass me. Unfortunately, no one was home. He took that opportunity to prowl around, looking for anything he might find that could later be used against me if I chose to divorce him. He ransacked the room in which I slept, and under the mattress he found the letters that Joe had written me.

Judging from Lee's reaction when he called that night to tell me he had found them, they were not the kind of letters he had expected. The words on the pages were not just words of love, but words of support, fully understanding about the mess my life was in. In those letters, Joe had not only talked of love but of ways in which I might try to help myself stay strong.

Two days later, Lee was back at my father's house, and, again, no one was home. This time he waited impatiently for me to come home. As soon as I walked through the door, he started flashing my cherished letters in my face and threatening to turn them over to a lawyer to be used in court if I ever tried divorcing him. He said he was going to hold onto them for collateral. We had not talked of divorce, but I knew that was the next step and apparently he did too, for he had mentioned the word more than once. He told me I'd never get a divorce from him, and if I tried, he'd make my life a living hell.

I knew losing his wife and children was a severe blow to his pride and ego. In his mind, it was one thing for his wife to take up with another man while we were separated, but quite another for her to take up with a *white* man. He was a man stuck in the mentality of the times; a man could disrespect his wife in any way he chose, yet a woman was never supposed to disrespect her husband. A man could cheat, but not a wife. A man could go out and get drunk and make a fool of himself, but it was shameful if a wife did the same thing. A man could take out his hostilities on his wife, but God forbid if a wife ever raised her hand to her husband. Women were nothing more than possessions to men like Lee.

Joe's and my relationship was sizzling hot, and we were determined to be together despite the odds against us. We had long since stopped hiding our feelings for each other. We tried to be more discreet for Lee's sake. I knew Lee was relentlessly teased by his friends and people who knew him, which made his obsession over my relationship with Joe even more desperate. He told me that some of his friends had said, "Man, I wouldn't let no white man come in here and take my wife. You have to stand up and be a man." He was like a madman on a mission. In the end, that obsession caused him to lose the job that he had finally acquired.

He missed too much time from work following Joe and me around. He seemed to be everywhere.

As Joe's and my relationship blossomed, the physical and emotional stress grew progressively worse. At one point, I became so paranoid that whenever I saw two people whispering, I immediately assumed they were talking about us. If it had not been for Joe's strength, I truly don't know if I would have had the courage to go on. My friends began to drift away. The whole town seemed to have turned against me. I strived to find a way to survive this bold interference into my private life.

My family, by then, had heard rumors about Joe and me. When they started asking questions, I felt compelled to tell them the truth. Up until then, I had not sat down and discussed my relationship with anyone in my family. They questioned whether I'd be able to deal with all the obstacles that I surely would face and whether I could trust Joe, because, after all, he was *white*! At first, they were upset, but reluctantly gave in once they learned how much I had grown to love him.

Somehow, the relationship felt right after I surmounted the fact that he was of another race. As we continued to gain insight into each other, his color became less and less an issue, because I knew in my heart that he was the man that God had sent for me. I guess when I prayed and asked for a good man to be sent to me, I had not been specific enough. I got the good man; he just didn't come wrapped in the package that I thought he would. But I was wise enough to know who he was.

I knew my family loved me, even though this relationship put them in an awkward situation. I stayed away from my sister Ruth, because I didn't want to create problems between her and her husband. He had made it clear he didn't want anything to do with either Joe or me.

Louetta wasn't married so we did spend some time with her and her children on occasion. Dot's husband, Leroy, was the first one in my family to really welcome Joe. One evening Joe took me over to Dot's house to pick up something. When we drove up, I told him to stay in the car and I'd run in to get whatever it was I was picking up and I'd be right out. I knocked on the door, and Leroy answered it but he could see around me that Joe was waiting in the car. He said, "Come on in; Dot is in the back."

I went to the sitting room where Dot was, and as Dot and I started chatting, we heard Leroy talking to someone in the living room. We both looked at each other, astonished. I recognized Joe's voice immediately. I became very nervous, not sure how Dot was going to react to having Joe in her home. We both got up about the same time, me sprinting ahead of her to usher Joe out before any commotion could get started.

By the time Dot entered, Leroy stood and announced that he had invited Joe in. That eased some of the tension that I was feeling because I wasn't sure how Joe ended up sitting in their living room. Dot and I sat down to join them. The conversation was strained. I can't even remember what we talked about, probably not much. The only thing I do remember vividly is being relieved to be out of the house. Once in the car Joe told me that Leroy had come out and invited him in. That visit broke the ice, and the two formed a very civil relationship from that.

My family's main concern was how hard my life would become if I continued to be involved with a white man. I couldn't think that far ahead; I had to deal with the now. I just wanted my family to give our love a chance and get to know Joe as I had. Finally, after many discussions back and forth, they did guardedly give in and became willing to meet me halfway, which was all I could ask of them.

Joe and I decided to stop seeing each other altogether until I got a divorce. This decision came in the wake of a local killing spree in which a man shot nine people, killing eight of them. The man had intended to kill his wife's whole family, from grown-ups to children. He shot each family member in the head while they were sleeping in their beds. That act of murderous rage terrified us because we didn't know what frame of mind Lee was in, or what he might do next. As it was, he was following us around all the time. Would he get any ideas from this tragedy? My biggest fear was wondering if he was capable of murder, too. Joe and my family feared for my safety.

Joe and I talked it over and thought it might be better for me to take the children and leave town for a while. Two weeks later, Joe bought tickets for us to go by train to Chicago to stay with my brother. While there, I decided to apply for a job. I had the skills as I had just recently finished a secretarial course. I scanned the local newspaper want ads and saw an ad with a law firm that caught my eye. I called and set up an interview. The firm consisted of two brothers looking for someone who could type up to fifty words per minute. Another requirement was someone who could work alone, and was very skillful in taking directions. After the interview, they thought I'd be the perfect candidate. I was offered the job that day. I was terribly excited about being offered a job but after two months of snow and cold, I began to miss the warmer climate in Mississippi, and I missed Joe as well. Needless to say, I didn't take the job but decided to go home instead. I did go back with a new determination to face Lee and make preparations to get a divorce.

The first Sunday after my return, Joe, Nikki, Shea, and I

went to visit my sister Louetta and her children in Port Gibson. While we were there, Joe and I agreed to watch her children while she ran some errands. No more than ten minutes after she had gone, we heard a familiar voice yelling outside the door, "Tootise, Tootise, you in there?"

I froze with fear. It was Lee. Apparently he had followed us there and watched the house until Louetta left. He didn't knock; he just kicked the door down, walked in and struck Joe with his fist, shouting, "This really feels good. I've always wanted to hit a white man!" He shoved me to the floor. The children were hysterical, but that didn't stop him.

Louetta arrived home, took a horrified look around at what had happened, and called the police, who quickly responded. They escorted Lee outside and asked my sister if she wanted to press charges. She refused, so not much could be done. She said she did this because Lee was her brother-in-law, not because she was afraid of him. In fact, she said she felt sorry for him. My family still wasn't quite settled on my dating. The police gave him a stern warning and let him go.

On the way home, Lee was waiting for us. He was parked on a side road and followed us as we passed by, all the way home with Nikki and Shea cowering in the back seat. Nothing else happened that day, but his menacing presence was intimidating enough.

A similar incident happened another time when we were visiting a family Joe knew in Natchez. He was very close to the Larry family because he had lived with them briefly during his days of working with the voter registration drive. They invited us down for dinner. As we were eating and talking, a knock sounded at the door, and there was Lee. He had followed us again. At least this time he chose to knock on the door rather than kicking it in.

Everyone at the table already knew who he was. Jake Larry, our host, asked him to please leave, adding that he would have him arrested if he didn't. Lee didn't ignore his warning because, unlike my sister, Jake would have had him arrested and would have filed trespassing charges against him. Looking through the screen door he yelled at me, "Tootise, I want my rings back!"

How embarrassing. But I pulled the rings off right then and there and threw them toward the door. He picked up the rings and left.

6
The Divorce

In the state of Mississippi, in 1974, there was no such thing as a no-fault divorce. A reason for a divorce had to be presented, one that could be proven beyond a shadow of a doubt. And before the court would allow a case to be heard, one had to have a witness, someone who would testify on behalf of the plaintiff to corroborate on the evidence presented.

My divorce settlement also consisted of a custody suit. Lee was trying to prove to the court that I was an unfit mother. His only proof was that I was going with a white man, but in Lee's mind, that was proof enough. He still had my letters. His first disappointment came when he presented the letters to his lawyer, in the hopes of strengthening his case, and his lawyer advised him the judge would take a dim view of his stealing them. What he had tried to hold over my head for so long proved to be more of a letdown than an asset to his case.

I had problems too, namely difficulty finding someone who would testify as my witness. After all, I had done the forbidden, taken up with a white man publicly, and everyone in town had his or her nose in my business. I'd become the talk of the town. Tongues wagged more than a dog's tail. I was not the first black woman to ever become involved with a white man; others just did it behind closed doors. All anyone had to do was look around and see all the different colors of children to know that there was a whole lot of race mixing going on. The people who condemned me so harshly seemed to be the same ones with the most to hide. It infuriated me to be ostracized by people I thought I knew.

When my first court date came up, I had my witness lined up along with my uninterested court-appointed attorney. My witness, a black woman who had previously assured me of her friendship, had promised to stand with me and testify. On the day of my court appearance, I got there early, went in, and sat down to wait for her. Fifteen minutes passed, and still no witness. I began looking around anxiously, knowing how much was riding on this person. The judge banged his gavel, saying if my witness didn't show up in the next five minutes, my hearing would have to be postponed until the next divorce court date.

My witness never showed up, and when I next saw her, she ignored me, acting as though nothing had happened. While he couldn't rule on the divorce, the judge did make a decision about our children on that first court appearance. He said that I was to have them for two weeks, and Lee would get them for two weeks. That arrangement was to be followed until the next hearing. A final decision, in the best interest of the children, would be made when the divorce was granted.

At that time in Mississippi, divorce court was held every quarter, or four times a year. While I was waiting for the next court date, the judge didn't know I only got to see my children for two weeks. When I gave them to Lee as ordered by the court, he refused to give them back when his two weeks were up. I'd call and ask him to bring them to me, but he'd laugh and tell me that I had no time for my children; I only had time for my white lover. I was furious with him. He wouldn't allow me to see our children or talk to them on the phone.

The second time we went to court, I had not seen my children for well over four months. I was becoming physically ill from all the stress and strain. This time I had a different court-appointed attorney, but one just as unconcerned as the first one. Just when I thought I had everything ready, my second witness, another black woman, failed to show up. I knew what that meant: the case would be put off again for another four months or longer, depending on the judge. With a heavy heart, I got up and walked out of the courtroom. I never contacted the second person to ask why. Like the first one, it was obvious. No one wanted Lee to see them standing up for me. This witness thing was going to be a little more difficult than I anticipated.

I was now nearing exhaustion and feeling deeply humiliated, not only by the two witnesses who stood me up, but also by the impersonal way I was being treated in court. Lee's lawyer talked with the judge and other court officials about me as if I weren't there. My court-appointed lawyers merely represented me because they were told to do so. The courtroom was full of spectators at each hearing, waiting to grab an earful. Also, each time the divorce was put off I had to live with the vicious and malicious gossip that followed. More paranoia set in.

The most gossip stemmed from the fact that I was leaving my husband for a white man and trying to take his children away from him. Lee had a lot of people fooled about our relationship and his philandering ways. He made it sound as though everything that had happened was my fault and he was the innocent victim. He even had some people thinking I really didn't want my children. My actions, based on one man's perception, were being judged cruelly by the public.

Between the first and second court dates, I went without seeing Nikki and Shea for over seven months. When I thought I just couldn't stand it any longer, I borrowed my father's car and went to my in-laws' house to try and see my children. As soon as Lee's family saw me drive up and get out of the car, they demanded that I leave immediately, shouting, "Get off our property! Get off now, and don't ever set foot on it again."

I stood there in shock. I got back in the car and drove off with tears running down my face. Shortly after that episode, I learned they had obtained a restraining order from the sheriff's department to keep me away. His parents told me that as long as they had the kids, I was not to try to see them again.

Despite the fact that Lee was violating the judge's two-week visitation rights, the sheriff (of course the sheriff was white) issued the restraining order and told me that I'd be arrested and thrown in jail if I disobeyed it. Once again, the man in question didn't have to obey the courts. I was the one treated as if I had broken the law and had ignored the judge's ruling.

I stayed away because I didn't want Lee's family to press charges against me. Certainly it wouldn't have been in my favor to get arrested and thrown in jail, especially since I was fighting for custody of our kids. I couldn't turn to law enforcement for help because they sided with Lee and his family. Amidst all the mayhem, I had to stay alert at all times because Lee was constantly up to some kind of evil.

As time went on, even with Joe's support, I began to feel very lonely. It was almost as if the whole town was against me. Joe was certainly my pillar of strength, but it would have helped if I had more family support. They wanted nothing to do with the case, never showing up in court for moral support, and insisting what I'd done was bringing too much unwanted attention. They were concerned for my well-being and my safety, but my siblings had their own families to consider. They, too, were wounded by the vicious gossip that circulated around town. It not only tainted me but, by association, tainted them and their families as well.

My family's fears for my safety were not completely unfounded. Despite the fact that the Civil Rights Movement had brought about many positive changes in the way blacks were being treated in Fayette, many other small, rural towns still continued to regard blacks as second-class citizens. A black person could be thrown in jail without an explanation, found dead in his cell the next day, and the death labeled a suicide.

Widely believed in lots of black communities was that any black person who challenged the laws of authority would be harassed or killed. As generations of Mississippi blacks had learned, there was still virtually no end to the physical and psychological brutality of a southern jail. Even when nothing happened, the possibility of a threat of violence or even death at the hands of the police left most people vulnerable in their custody. The movement had tried to change all of that, but in some smaller towns, the attempts had been unsuccessful. The mere prospect of going to jail still terrified many southern blacks.

Joe and I didn't spend a lot of time together, still honoring our promise to keep our relationship to a minimum. The few times we did, we tried to do something special. On one of those special occasions, we took a long drive to get away from all the worry and stress. We needed to clear our heads and try to think rationally about the state our lives were in.

We ended up back in Brookhaven, a small, redneck town. It was not our destination when we started out, but that's where we were around 11:00 a.m., when we felt the beginning of hunger pains growling around in our stomachs.

Brookhaven was also considered KKK territory, a place where blacks supposedly still knew their place. People used to say that many rednecks and peckerwoods lived in that part of the state. The potential for violence in small towns such as Brookhaven was very strong. However, that didn't occur to us at the time. Getting something to eat was at the forefront of our minds.

We spotted a little café on the side of a hill with a parking lot full of cars. We drove up and got out of the car. Peering into the window, we saw it was full of customers as well. Everyone seemed to be talking and having a good time. One could smell the aroma from outside, which made the rumblings in our bellies more evident. We decided to go in for lunch. Standing outside the door, the noise sounded like the buzz from an active beehive, but when we walked in, the atmosphere instantaneously changed from friendly to unfriendly. The noise stopped abruptly. Forks were frozen in midair. All eyes were suddenly upon us.

A sign on the counter read, "Please seat yourself." Hesitantly, we weaved through aisles around the tables until we found one close to the kitchen and sat down. Every time we went out in those days, we'd always try to sit near the kitchen. I wanted to see who was preparing the food, if possible. I was trying to see if the cook was black or white. If it was a black cook, then I felt a little safer about eating the food. I was always afraid that a white cook might spit on my food before serving it.

Everyone was looking at us. The room was perfectly quiet. Six policemen sat at a nearby table, but that didn't make us feel any safer. Sitting among those unfriendly faces, I began to worry about our safety. No one back home knew of our whereabouts.

As we were sitting there waiting, I wondered what we'd

do if we were refused service, which by now seemed to be a very real possibility. Finally, a black waitress came out of the kitchen. I breathed a sigh of relief, thinking that she was coming to take our order. She ignored us and merely went around refilling coffee cups, taking care of the customers who had already been served.

The waitress and some of the other employees knew we were there, because when we first walked in and things got quiet so fast, I saw them peeking through a small window in the kitchen door, staring as we found seats. It looked as if we weren't going to be served after all. As annoyed as I was with that black waitress, I understood the pressure she must have been feeling. Even if she wanted to serve us, she must have felt some anxiety over what was happening and was probably afraid of losing her job.

I wanted to leave, but Joe insisted that we stay until we were served. He was very headstrong when it came to our rights. I wasn't so sure I could eat even if we did get food. We sat there for what seemed like an eternity. It was probably no more than about forty-five minutes. Finally, the same black waitress who earlier filled the coffee cups came up to our table to take our orders. In a very dry and sullen voice she asked, "What can I get for you today?"

The air was really thick in that café that morning, and not just from all the smokers. I felt all eyes were staring at us. By now some of the customers had begun to talk again, only in much lower tones than before. We couldn't make out what anyone was saying, but it was very obvious that no one seemed to feel at ease with us around.

After another forty-five minutes passed, our food finally arrived. By then I had completely lost my appetite. Besides that, I was too tense to eat. Somehow, I managed to eat a small portion of the meal, with Joe finishing his off completely. We paid the check and left.

The odd thing I noticed that morning was no one seemed in a hurry to leave the restaurant. Not a single soul got up to leave while we were there, not even the six policemen. I imagine when we left we must have given them a lot to speculate about. We were hardly out the door before the buzz started up again.

We might have been too tense to talk when we were in the café, but we had plenty to talk about on the way home. In situations like that, I was always afraid for Joe more than for myself, because it was known that he had come to Mississippi to work with the voter registration. The presence of civil rights workers from the North had incited a number of rednecks to violence in some parts of the state.

As it was, we had more than rednecks to worry about. Lee seemed determined to carry on his frightening and intimidating confrontations. I went to the Evers Lounge one night, something I rarely did any more. Joe worked at the lounge part time, as did some other white people who had previously worked for the mayor in his voter registration drive or as part of his campaign staff. Mayor Evers believed that having white presence working in a black establishment and waiting on black customers was quite a reversal from the way things used to be.

I knew I'd see Joe at the lounge. I thought it would give us a chance to talk in between his waiting on customers. I asked my father to give me a ride there and I'd get Joe to bring me home. My plans were to have a few dances, loosen up, and enjoy myself. I took a seat at a far back table trying to be as inconspicuous as possible. When Joe noticed I was there, he came over, we chatted, and I told him I'd be waiting to get a ride home with him. He brought me a Coke and told me to enjoy. It was unusually busy that night, which gave us very little time to do much talking. We did manage a few bits and pieces of conversation, but lots of eye contact. To this day, I still believe someone saw me and used the pay phone to call Lee and tell him I was there.

I had a wonderful time. I even had a few dances. When the place closed, Joe and I left for home. We had to drive down a long, winding dirt road with lots of little roads off to the side. Years before, most of those little roads led somewhere, to someone's house or to a corn or cotton field. Now the houses were all gone, and hardly anyone was farming anymore. The roads were overgrown. As we were driving down the main road, Lee popped out from one of those narrow side roads with lights blaring, wildly honking his car horn.

We were really caught off guard. This was not like the day he followed us to Port Gibson. This time he was chasing us and driving very recklessly and dangerously. He couldn't get his car around us, but he did stay very close behind, weaving in and out. Thank goodness we lived on a road with no or little traffic. That night, the road was completely deserted.

Joe drove as fast as he dared, trying to stay ahead of him, but he was at a disadvantage. Having driven that road often, Lee knew where all the sharp curves were, where to slow down, and where to drive faster. This enabled him to keep right on our bumper. I could do nothing but sit in shame and fright. I was certain Lee meant to kill us that night.

When we approached the road that would have taken us to my father's house, we were too afraid to slow down to make the turn. Rocks were flying, dust almost making it impossible to see. We just kept going. I knew the road we were on would eventually lead to a paved one, which would lead us back into town.

When we reached the paved road, we really took off. Still, Lee managed to pass us and get ahead. He tried to block us by putting his car crosswise on the road. Joe, with his quick thinking, managed to drive off the shoulder around the car and avoid hitting him. That only made it worse. Lee thought he had us. When I looked back in the rearview mirror, his car was spinning around in the road out of control. It took him a minute to get it straight enough to drive again. When he did, he started chasing us with a vengeance. The time it took him to get his car straightened up gave us a chance to get far enough ahead so he couldn't catch us. Joe drove me to my friend Macy Talbot's house. She was the only person I knew who would take me in without questions. After he dropped me off, he went on to Father Morrissey's house, where he was staying.

Sometimes I thought Lee had a death wish, but not necessarily his own. I shudder to think what Lee might have done had he been able to trap us.

I was almost at my wit's end after the interminable divorce hearings and custody battle, and I didn't know which way to turn. I had tried to hire a private attorney: two, in fact, but I barely made it past my name. When I stated my name, their reception turned chilly, right away, and it was obvious my reputation had preceded me. Both attorneys suddenly realized their present caseloads prevented them from taking on anything that would require so much attention.

My friend Macy Talbot recommended a white attorney by the name of Fred Burgess. She said she had recently worked with him on a black/white issue and felt that he might be able to help me. She stated that he also worked with the ACLU. She asked, "Would you like his phone number?" She also sensed my hesitation. Encouragingly she said, "It's surely worth a try, Martha." I had to agree with her because so far I hadn't made any progress, and I was beginning to feel very disheartened.

I called Mr. Burgess's office and made an appointment to see him the very next day. Already feeling insecure, I had prepared myself for another rejection. I couldn't imagine why Mr. Burgess would want to help me, but I was desperate. When I walked into his office, he stood, introduced himself, and offered me a seat. I was very impressed by this small gesture of good manners after the way I had been treated by the other two lawyers I'd approached. They'd barely noticed my presence, let alone offered me a seat.

Then I noticed how big and tall Mr. Burgess was. His height was very intimidating. I cautiously sat down, trying to think what to say that would make this man want to take my case. As I sat there staring at him, trying to will my mouth to speak, I was thinking there was no way this redneck-looking man could possibly want to help me. His long silence only increased my anxiety.

Mr. Burgess, who already knew who I was and why I was there, said he had done some checking around since he received my call. Luckily for me, this spared me from having to give him the details of my case, because my mouth felt as dry as the Sahara desert. I began to think, just maybe, I'd found an attorney at last. Then my hopes were crushed when he said that he would soon be leaving private practice to become a district judge. He, therefore, would be unable to take my case.

It took all of my strength to sit there and hold back the tears that were threatening to spill over. Joe and I had talked this over, and we both agreed that it might be better if I went in alone. At that moment, though, I was wishing Joe had been there with me instead of outside waiting. Somehow, I think we both thought that if we weren't seen together, then I'd have a better chance.

Sitting there with all these thoughts going around my head, I barely heard him when he said, "However, I have a friend, Frank Walden, another local attorney, willing to talk to you." This new attorney was willing to see me as soon as I left his office. He said he had already called and filled Mr. Walden in on the case and that he was expecting me. When I stood to leave, Mr. Burgess stood and said, "Martha, I can't be your attorney, but I will be the judge presiding over your case, so try not to worry so much." We shook hands on my departure. Hearing those words made me feel lightheaded. I savored every word Fred Burgess had said to me, especially his last ones.

I felt a sliver of hope, for this man had, indeed, given me some encouragement. His words had sent a fresh surge of adrenaline pumping through my veins. I was almost skipping to the car as I shared every detail of that conversation with Joe. He, too, felt delightedly hopeful. It had been a long time since I'd felt that lighthearted.

With directions in hand, Joe and I found our way to Mr. Walden's office. When I knocked on the door, Mr. Walden greeted me with a warm smile and a firm, but friendly, handshake. Joe went in with me. We didn't feel so fearful of being seen together this time. Mr. Walden pulled up two big black leather chairs close to his desk for Joe and me to sit down. He shuffled a few papers around on his desk before taking a clean notepad out as if he was going to jot down notes. Then he asked me to give him my story in my own words. As I spoke, I noticed he was, in fact, jotting on that note pad. Of course, he had heard all the rumors but wanted to hear what

I had to say. I sat across from that stranger and poured my heart out to him, discovering that I had no trouble talking in his office.

After hearing my story, Mr. Walden immediately said he would take my case. He did caution me that this was going to be a tough and messy divorce, but he said I had suffered enough. He explained all the things that probably would happen. He said my case would not be like a regular divorce case, because my husband was fighting against it so strongly and also demanding custody of our children.

Mr. Walden told me that the main reason why this case was going to be a difficult one was because a black man was accusing a white man of breaking up his family and trying to take his children away from him. Thus, in a predominantly black town deep in the rural south, Lee would draw sympathy from the hometown folks. My case was going to draw attention no matter what, he said. Mr. Walden persistently asked if Joe and I were up to the challenge. We both agreed we were. He then told us that this was not only going to affect my life but Joe's as well. He wanted us to understand, right up front, what we were up against.

Mr. Walden did ease some of my fears. He said, "Martha, as long you and Joe understand, in the end, you'll get the results you want; it's getting there that's going to be the rough part." He advised me to let Lee keep the children for now until all of this was over, which, of course, was a big disappointment to me.

"You'll find it hard at first," he continued. "I sympathize, but I think it's the best arrangement as far as the children are concerned." He then told me, "You should take this free time and prepare yourself for their return." He added, "This delay, while a letdown, will give you an opportunity to put some balance in your life and build a more stable environment for the children as well as for yourself."

For the next few months, while waiting for yet another court date, I had time to think. I realized I needed a plan, and much more than anything else, a dependable witness, one who would not be afraid of my soon-to-be ex-husband. When I told Mr. Walden, he agreed. He said we needed to make some changes in our strategy to enhance the chance for a more positive outcome. He had three very good recommendations. First, we should ask to have the next hearing moved to Natchez, Adams County. He felt that I wouldn't receive a fair hearing in my hometown.

Secondly, he would request that his friend Fred Burgess be the presiding judge over my case, which would be in my favor. While Mr. Walden said he couldn't make any promises, he felt sure that I would be judged fairly based on the evidence that was presented.

And, finally, he wanted the case to be heard in closed court, open only to the plaintiff, the defendant, their families, and the witnesses. This sounded almost too good to be true. No more snickering, staring, and gloating. I didn't know it was possible to have my hearing in a closed court. The other two court-appointed lawyers never even talked to me, let alone made any kind of suggestions.

I still had to go through the process of finding a reliable witness. I wracked my brains trying to come up with someone I thought would be dependable. I asked Gilda, a lady I knew from my younger years. We had played together as children. We didn't see each other very often, nor were we good friends, but we had always maintained a speaking relationship. I saw her uptown, and we stopped to chat. As we were talking, I just simply asked her if she would consider being a witness in my divorce case. I told her about the other two and what had happened. To my surprise she said yes, and then stated, "I heard how the others stood you up. I'm not afraid of Lee; I'll do it." She assured me she would be there. She said, "Just let me know the date, time, and where to meet you." With those words, we parted ways, but deep in my gut I felt she'd come through for me.

And she did. I was finally granted my divorce in October 1974. I was also able to take my children home that day from the courthouse. It wasn't a pleasant experience because Lee's parents didn't want to give them up. The judge (Fred Burgess) also granted me sole custody of our children with Lee having two supervised weekends a month for visitation. Mr. Walden told me later that Lee had inadvertently helped my case with all of his outrageous actions in the past.

7
My Marriage to Joe

The first time Joe asked me to marry him, I said, "No." I explained to him that my divorce had only been final for a few weeks. I wanted a taste of freedom. It was just way too soon for me to leap into another marriage. Also, I had my children to consider as well. I worried about how our relationship was going to affect them. Nikki and Shea were five and three and even at that age they were well aware that something was going on. They had met Joe several times and knew he was different but didn't quite understand what that difference was. They didn't comprehend the color barrier.

When Joe explained to me we'd have fewer problems if we got married—and the sooner the better—it all made sense. He worried about having two young children involved in a courtship like ours, and felt that once we got married, no one could question our love or our commitment to each other. That would make us a lot safer as a family. He also said that if I wasn't ready to marry him, then we should stop seeing each other until I was willing to make a stronger commitment to our relationship.

I certainly didn't want to do that! I did want to marry him, just not so soon. I saw the wisdom in what he said, and we immediately started making plans to get married. There would be no formal wedding, just a simple civil ceremony.

We went to the local health department to have blood tests done, and when the results came back, we went to the courthouse in Fayette to apply for a license. The city clerk saw us as we walked in, and he looked very uncomfortable. I was sure someone from the health department had called and given him advance warning. We were infamous, after all; everyone in town knew who we were, and many people within the surrounding towns knew of us. He looked away and started shuffling papers on his desk as if he was too busy to look up. Clearing his throat, he tried very hard to ignore us.

We just stood there, waiting for him to acknowledge our presence. When he didn't, Joe stated that we had come to apply for a marriage license. After much delay, he reluctantly looked up and asked our names and address. We had already bought a mobile home, which was all set up, waiting for us to move in. Joe had it moved to a piece of rental property in Natchez owned by the Larry family.

When we gave an out-of-town address, it was hard not to see the relief on the man's face; we had provided him with an excuse. Without even looking at us, he stood and announced that we had to have a local address to apply for a marriage license, and since we lived in Natchez, he couldn't do anything for us in Fayette. He then turned, walked into a back room, and closed the door behind him.

The Natchez courthouse was much bigger than Fayette's, which made it seem much more unapproachable. There were so many people bustling around. They were all dressed up. The men were in suits and ties, while the women wore high-heeled shoes and dark, flattering suits. And they were all white. The only black people I saw that morning were the ones with mops and brooms cleaning the hallways, stopping to let the white people pass.

When Joe and I walked past together, they stopped and stared. We proceeded down a long, wide, tiled hallway with very shiny floors. After reading almost every title above the big, polished wooden doors, we finally found the one with city clerk written on it.

We entered, but our presence was not acknowledged. The woman behind the desk, like the man in Fayette, never looked up. She was busy reading the newspaper. We stood by her desk and waited for a few minutes. We knew by now that she wasn't going to look at us. Again, Joe stated why we were there, talking to a bent head. When he finished, she got up, laid the paper down, and without a mere glance, walked over to a file cabinet, took out some legal papers, and threw them on her desk in our direction. "Fill these out," she said and then sat back down and continued to read her paper. We went to a small table in the corner and filled out the papers, going over them thoroughly to be sure we didn't miss a thing. When we were done, we walked up and put the papers back on her desk. While holding the newspaper in one hand and our papers in the other, she started to look them over. I guess she decided she needed to be more focused, for she laid down the newspaper and turned her full attention to the filled-out papers. She carefully read them, as if hoping to find some small detail that we might have overlooked. She remained edgy and unfriendly.

A few minutes lapsed without anything being said. The room was incredibly quiet. Finally, she said, "I don't know which book to put you in, the *colored* book or the *white* book." With that comment, she disappeared into another room, and we didn't see her for over a half hour. When she came back, she had a smirk on her face as she blurted out, "I'll just have to put you both in the *colored* book!"

With that, she hauled out a big, dark-reddish, well-worn book, found the correct page, and told us to sign our names.

She stamped our paperwork and handed a piece of paper back to us, returned to her seat, picked up the newspaper, and continued to read without saying another word.

I bit my tongue to avoid speaking what I felt. What should have taken an hour at most had taken more than three to complete. We left the courthouse hungry and fatigued. From there we went to Mazique's, a black-owned cafe, to have something to eat and try to make plans for our upcoming marriage. It wasn't just setting a date; it was also finding someone willing to marry us. Over lunch, we tried to think of a minister but couldn't come up with anyone. Father Morrissey would have gladly married us, but being a Catholic priest, he couldn't marry anyone who had been divorced.

I suggested that we might ask the minister of the church I attended. He had been very involved in the Civil Rights Movement which, in our opinion, would make him a more liberal minister. When I tried to contact my minister, I learned that he was out of town, and no one seemed to know exactly when he would be returning. However, I was informed that he did have a cousin who was also a minister and that he might be willing to marry us. I related this information to Father, and he helped us locate Reverend Robert Howard.

When I called Reverend Howard and asked if he would marry us, he said, "Yes, I'll be happy to perform the ceremony." He added, "Just let me know the date and details." I thanked him profusely and told him that I would get back to him as soon as we had finalized our plans. Joe and I agreed it would not be wise to have a big wedding. Besides, who would we invite? Except for my family, most people had shied completely away from us by then, even the so-called friends. I really didn't think anyone in my family would have attended either.

We decided it would be better to get married at night rather than during the day, and we shouldn't get married in Fayette. We certainly didn't want to draw any more unwanted attention.

Joe wanted to get married under a gazebo overlooking the Mississippi River down on the bluff in Natchez. I didn't care where we got married as long as we could be together with the children, in seclusion.

We needed two witnesses to stand up for us, but instead of asking someone we knew really well and taking the chance of being turned down, we asked Grace and Kelly, a white couple who worked at the supermarket with Joe and were the only white couple who had befriended us from the start. They lived a few miles north of Natchez in the small town of Washington and said they'd be happy to stand up for us.

Everything was planned and set for the Wednesday before Thanksgiving, November 27, 1974. We called Reverend Howard and told him of our plans. We told him we had set the time for 8:00 p.m. "I'll see you then," he said.

The five of us met at the bandstand under a very bright full moon. As we were nervously standing there, with the wind blowing a chilly breeze around us, I was thinking, "This is where my new life begins." We hadn't planned a honeymoon; that would come later, if at all. Right then, I just wanted to escape to our new mobile home and try to forget about all the ugliness that had led up to that point. After the brief ceremony, we thanked Reverend Howard and the Kellys, said our good-byes, and left. We picked up the children from the Larrys, who had been watching them for us during our brief ceremony, and went to our new home.

We started out as husband and wife at 1258 Daisy Street, Natchez, Mississippi. Joe had talked about our moving to California, where we'd more likely have fewer problems once we were married. He said it was a much more liberal state than most. Interracial marriages were accepted there. That conversation never got much past the talking stage. It had never occurred to me to live any place other than Mississippi, for it was the only place I knew. I couldn't imagine life away from my family. Although we had endured many unnecessary hardships in Mississippi, I wasn't ready to up and move away. Fayette was my home, and if I couldn't live there, then I surely wanted to live nearby.

Daisy Street ended where we lived, at the bottom of a steep hill, which gave us the privacy that I had craved for so long. There were no other houses under the hill, just ours. I was so worn out by then that I just wanted the four of us to go into hiding and live a cocoon-like existence. I kept to myself after we settled in, not wanting to get involved in anything that would force me to meet other people. But in reality, I knew we couldn't live in isolation forever, because Joe had to go to work, and the children had to go to school.

We still had Joe's parents to deal with. Up to this point, they had no idea what was going on in his personal life. They knew he had left college just before graduation to come to Mississippi as a volunteer to work in the Evers campaign, but that was about all. His parents weren't too happy about his skipping out on his graduation ceremony, but it was his decision to make. His mother, all along, was much more accepting of his coming south, but his father's attitude about race had been formed in his hometown, Macon, Georgia, and he had been totally against Joe's decision to work with voter registration, especially in Mississippi.

When we lived in Natchez, my children were able to attend a school where virtually no one knew them. The three of us together looked ordinary, a mother with her two children. I registered them at St. Mary's Cathedral, a private Catholic school which ranged from preschool through twelfth grade, without the staring and whispering. My goal was to get them settled before anyone found out about our private life. I know now my last name was a dead giveaway, being such an uncommon one in that part of the U.S.

Joe was still working at the supermarket six days a week in Fayette. He left home early mornings and returned late in the evenings. I lived a very low-profile life, usually staying home, going out only when necessary for school functions, doctors' appointments, etc. Sunday was usually family day. We took the kids on long drives to secluded parks to play and run around. We spent a lot of time on the Natchez Trace Parkway. We enjoyed many activities there alone, family picnics, playing softball, and other games. Almost everything we did back in those days involved just the four of us, mostly in remote places. That lifestyle soon became very lonesome for me as I realized that isolation wasn't the answer for a healthy lifestyle. Joe had his work, the kids had school, but I had no real outside interests for myself. Whenever the kids had some activity at school, I always attended alone. I was so afraid to meet new people for fear they would find out about my marriage. I was trying to hide it as if it were some deep, dark secret. Deep down, it was rejection that I was most afraid of.

As soon as school was out for the summer, I started going back to Fayette more and more to visit my sisters and their children. Nikki and Shea enjoyed being able to play with their cousins. We usually visited when their husbands were away at work so as not to cause problems. My brothers-in-law didn't want anything more to do with me once Joe and I got married. They really preferred I'd stay away from their homes altogether. Their rejection made me come to realize how important my family was to me and how much I missed and needed them.

Natchez was a paper mill town. Some days, the whole town smelled like rotten eggs. The unpleasant odor was hard to escape. It penetrated through closed doors and the closed windows of homes and cars. The whole town looked hazy, similar to the fog in Los Angeles. The citizens of Adams County seemed not to mind the offensive onslaught. The sulfurous odor drifted all the way to Fayette on a breezy day, but it still wasn't as strong as it was living there. Sometimes the stench lasted for days on end until a good rain came or until strong winds blew the air clean in again. That smell became part of our lives since we all had to breathe.

Six months after we moved away from Fayette, I was ready to move back home. I knew things wouldn't be any easier for us, but so far, nothing had been easy for Joe and me. My thinking was if I moved back, I would be closer to my family and I could more easily sneak in and visit my sisters whenever I wanted during the day.

I'm a very spontaneous person; once I make up my mind to do something, I like to do it immediately and get it over with. This hasn't always been in my best interest, but for the most part, it has worked. Now that I had made up my mind to move back, I could hardly wait for Joe to get home so I could tell him of my decision. I put the kids in their room to play right after dinner that night so we could be alone to talk. We chatted a bit, but I could hardly concentrate on what was being said. My thoughts were elsewhere. I wanted to get to the point of what was on my mind. Joe quickly noticed my lack of interest and asked what was wrong. Now would be as good a time as any to bring my decision out in the open.

I didn't beat around with small talk; I just blurted it out. "Joe, I want to move back home."

He looked at me wide-eyed, and said, "What! Just like that?"

"Of course, just like that," I said, wondering aloud, "how else would we do it?"

With concern on his face, he asked, "Martha, have you really thought this through? Are you sure this is something you really want to do?"

Well, I guess I hadn't really thought it through. I just knew it was what I wanted to do.

"Have you thought about how we'd go about making this move?" he asked.

I hadn't thought about that either, but I did suggest that we'd hire someone to pull our mobile home to Fayette, set it up, and we'd continue living as we were. In my haste, I didn't stop to think of all the details involved in making such a move. I forgot things such as where we would put our home once we moved it, who would pull it there, and how much it would cost. It was also imperative to have it anchored down because of the storms and hurricanes that we sometimes had. Those were major concerns, but minor ones in my mind, ones I knew somehow could be worked out. I just wanted to move home again.

Joe must have known how important this move was to me, because he did work out all the necessary details to have us moved, with very little help from me. He first purchased some land next to my father's FHA house. It was a beautiful piece of property with several big, old oak trees with one huge buckeye tree in the midst. The oak trees would provide shade, but the buckeye tree provided the most. There were at least two acres of green, lush lawn all around, with a spot between the oaks and the buckeye that was perfect for our home. Having an abundance of shade was very important when living in a mobile home. Most of them were made of tin, which caused them to become very hot in the summers. Ours did have central air conditioning for summers and heat for winters. It probably would have been almost impossible to live in a mobile home in such hot, humid weather without air conditioning.

After inquiring into the best way to have the trailer home moved, Joe paid the company that we had purchased it from to move us and to anchor it down. Everything went smoothly. I was home at last. In our new location, we made a walkway from our house to my father's house for convenience once we'd resettled. My father had long since befriended Joe. He was actually the first one in my family to welcome him. My relationship with my stepmother was about the same, except she seemed a bit more cordial. Being back home made me feel more relaxed, less alone and less uptight than I had been while living in Natchez. We lived in the countryside with only a very few houses scattered around fields of grass and trees. We knew all the neighbors, but everyone had privacy. It didn't take long for word to get around that we had moved back.

We kept the kids enrolled in school in Natchez. This was partly to protect them from the wagging tongues of our community. We didn't want them teased or mistreated because of our relationship. They remained there until Shea finished ninth grade, and Nikki, tenth. From there, they attended an all-girls boarding school in Atchison, Kansas. Even though the girls were born two years apart, they were only one year apart in school. That was due to the fact that Nikki started school when she was six years old and Shea started when she was five.

Thinking back, I have often wondered just how deep an

impact my marriage had on my children's lives. I had many misgivings about the course their lives were taking. However, I did believe that I was the master of my own fate; therefore, anything was possible if I wanted it badly enough. Believing that gave me the faith that, in the end, everything would work out for all of us. Even with the best intentions, it doesn't mean that I made all the right decisions concerning the people I loved the most.

Nikki and Shea became withdrawn and very insecure after my divorce from Lee. I didn't pay too much attention to their behavior at first, thinking that they needed more time to deal with the finality of my relationship with their father. I was somewhat skeptical but thought that as time wore on, they would adjust to our new life and see that, although I had remarried, I was still the same mother I had always been. I was hoping, too, that seeing how happy I was with Joe would give them some sense of security and belonging. They seemed fine up until we all moved in together.

Yet, the signs were always there, especially in the way Nikki repeatedly reached out for her dad. Whenever she saw him, her eyes became alive, and I saw the smile that she rarely displayed at home anymore. She was almost the little girl I remembered when we were living with Lee. She desperately wanted him to know he was the father she and Shea wanted in their lives, always speaking for her sister as well. Lee ignored them in his attempt to hurt me, which only made it worse for the children. But it made me more determined to help her and her sister understand that my marriage to another man wouldn't interfere with my relationships with them.

Whenever they did get a chance to see and talk to Lee, they asked him to take them to see their grandparents, his parents. Nikki had a close relationship with both his parents,

and that had been slashed out of her life. Everything familiar to them had been taken away, which caused them to put
most of the blame on Joe. I later learned that they blamed
me as well. Lee made promises but didn't keep them. I tried
never to speak a harsh word against him for fear of turning
them against me. I was forever making excuses about why
their daddy didn't show up, while trying to remain calm and
strong and not show my real feelings.

Nikki, more than Shea, remained distant and cold when
Joe was around. Shea just shyly looked on. Sometimes,
I caught Nikki staring at Joe with a look of pure hatred in
her eyes. She had convinced herself that if it hadn't been for
him, her father and I would still be together. In her mind, Joe
made everything about our lives complicated.

I found living in Fayette did have one big disadvantage; I
had to drive the twenty-five miles every day to get the children back and forth to school. Not only that, but almost everything else we wanted to do, except for buying groceries,
had to be done in Natchez as well. There was no movie the-
ater in Fayette and virtually no place to go out for a meal.

During those trips to Natchez, Joe and I were harassed relentlessly by the local and state law enforcement. Just about
every time we set out, we would look in the rearview mirror
and see a local or state police car following us. They usually
drove close behind us for several miles before turning off,
making sure we understood that we were being watched.

I was careful to drive within the speed limit, knowing I
was being watched. One morning, as I drove the children
to school I saw the familiar sight in my rearview mirror: a
squad car driven by a local white policeman. Although I
wasn't speeding, I still slowed down to a crawl. He trailed
my car for at least seven miles and then suddenly I heard a
voice on a loudspeaker saying, "Stop! Stop the car now!" This

time in the rearview mirror I saw flashing red lights and the policeman with his arm stuck out the window in a flagging position, instructing me to stop.

The children heard the voice as well and were very upset by the commotion. "Now just sit down and stay still," I told them in a trembling voice. "Nothing is going to happen." I don't think I was that assuring because I could see the anxiety on their faces. I pulled the car over to the side of the road and rolled down the window to hear more clearly what the officer was saying.

"Get out of the car now with your hands visible!" he shouted, still sitting in his car as he barked out the orders.

That made me really frightened, because I knew I'd done nothing wrong. The children started to cry. "Everything's going to be okay," I whispered to them as I slowly exited the car, trying to show my hands as clearly as possible.

"Walk around to the rear of the car and put your hands on the roof!" the policeman ordered.

I proceeded with caution, carefully doing everything he told me to do, worrying about my children. I didn't want to make the situation any worse or put them in any kind of danger.

As I stood there with my hands held high, people were driving by, gawking, waving, and blowing their car horns as they passed. I was humiliated—especially when I saw my friend Carleen Lloyd drive by on her way to work. I fought back tears.

Finally the policeman got out of his car. "You were speeding," he announced as he walked up to me. "Goin' thirty-seven in a thirty-five-mile speed zone."

I cringed as he moved closer and closer to me, but I didn't argue with him. As a matter of fact, I didn't say a word. I took the ticket and got back in my car.

"Oh, by the way," I heard him snicker as I walked around the car, "have a nice day," with a sneer in his voice.

I cleaned Nikki's and Shea's faces outside of the school before we got out of the car so they wouldn't appear to have been crying. Then I explained to them how important it was not to talk about what had happened with anyone at school or at home. I told them it would raise too many questions, and we needed to keep this our little secret. I had to go into the school with them and make up some plausible excuse for being late so they wouldn't be marked tardy.

I replayed that incident over and over in my mind while driving back home that morning. I decided I would just try to forget it and not tell anyone about what had happened. I had been treated unjustly because I was married to a white man. At that moment, I made up my mind not to tell Joe yet, maybe later, but for now it was too much to go over again. Besides, I knew he'd try and have something done, and that would just make the situation worse. I'm not sure what good it would have done anyway. I still had to drive the children to school every day.

It was about six months later before I could bring myself to talk about that incident. Joe was very surprised that I had kept it from him for so long. When he heard the story, he immediately wanted to have something done, just as I suspected. He wanted to at least try to find the policeman who was responsible, asking why I didn't get any details. I hadn't even thought of a detail during that time; I had been so frightened I had never really seen the policeman's face, for my back was turned to him with my hands stretched out on top of the car. In the end I talked Joe into just forgetting it altogether and moving on.

As it was, policemen followed us so often, it became a commonplace, albeit unnecessary, part of our lives. There were times when I briefly thought about leaving Joe, not because I didn't love him, but because life would have been a lot simpler if I had. Whenever some incident happened, it made me stop and think about his color. I tried not to see color with him, but it was hard not to when that was the main reason for the harassment we had to endure.

The world I had known and grown up in mysteriously disappeared when Joe came into my life. I lived in the same town, and I saw the same people that I had always known, but their attitudes toward me were totally different. It seemed like not too long ago, I could stop and have a chat with someone, a welcoming give-and-take with others, but after I became involved with Joe, I barely received a slight nod of the head from passersby. Most of those I had known all my life looked away when I walked by.

I had been naïve, for I sincerely believed being married would change how people treated me. The friendliness I'd experienced before now became twisted and ugly. For my own protection and self-preservation, I tried to cling more closely to those blacks I had once called friends, but I felt them pulling away too, whether consciously or unconsciously, not wanting to associate themselves with me for fear of retribution. I learned all too well that blacks can be just as racist as whites.

I harbored major resentment toward any past acquaintances who now appeared unfriendly towards me. I was devastated by the idea that other blacks no longer wanted me to be a part of their community. Couldn't they see I hadn't changed? Why had I been told I had to go to Jefferson High to fight for equality, to mix with the white race, to fight for desegregation, if my own people hated seeing me with a white man? What was equality all about if blacks couldn't see that Joe and I were equals?

I began to feel exposed and vulnerable with Joe, with no shield of any kind to thwart the sideways glances, the whispers, the wary looks in both black and white people's eyes. I wanted to scream at the top of my lungs to all of them, *"What the hell is wrong with you people? I'm still me, Martha, the same person you've known all your lives!"* I felt ostracized and learned to distrust the murmured greetings I received from the people I encountered, and I prayed that my children wouldn't ever have to experience the feelings I was experiencing. But I wasn't going to be a coward and run.

Ironically, while I was suffering racial discrimination on a very personal level, Mississippi was taking important steps toward racial equality. New changes in the law, through pressure and negotiation, had allowed the black man to step outside of "his place" and forced the white man to realize that no drastic effects would be suffered from eating in a restaurant with a black person, or from integrating schools, or from offering justice for all.

Still, when it came time to go to the polls, some blacks continued to show fear. Georgia representatives Julian Bond and John Lewis made a tour of our state in an effort to stimulate registration of black voters.

Even though Mayor Evers lost the gubernatorial election, he had achieved his secondary goal of surviving the election as a bona fide candidate for governor. I had never known that much dignity before. It was totally exhilarating. I felt that we, as blacks, had finally earned that sense of independence that comes with being a free people. The mayor had taught us how to avoid being intimidated by the whites at the polls.

We now had our very first apartment complex, the Martin Luther King Apartments, and we had the Evers Restaurant and Lounge, into which he brought professional and local entertainment. Tyrone Davis seemed to be the town's favorite. He was a singer, originally from Greenville, Mississippi. Though his music career took off in the North, he was very popular in the South. He had such hits as "Turn Back the Hands of Time," "Baby, Can I Change Your Mind?" and "A Woman Needs to be Loved." "Turn Back the Hands of Time" was one of my favorites; if only I could do just that.

The mayor had educated us on how to obtain loans for housing, small businesses, and farm equipment. A vocational school had been built. During the day, the school was used for regular classes for the students, but it initiated night classes for adults who could not read or write or for those who just wanted to further their education. It was the school I had attended, taking a typing and business course. The adults were taught skills or trades that would enable them to seek better jobs.

The social event of the year was the Medgar Evers Homecoming, in honor of Charles Evers's brother, which took months to plan and a great deal of time and energy to carry off. The result could be compared to any big gala held in New York City, ending with ballroom dancing.

It was always held on the first weekend of June in observance of Medgar's death on June 12, 1963. Usually the festivities got under way on Thursday and lasted throughout the weekend, ending on the following Monday. That event made the townspeople buzz with excitement. We never knew who we might see at those functions. The guest list was usually a very impressive one.

Security was beefed up during that time due to all the celebrities who flew in just for the occasion. The event would surely be of interest to avid KKK members as well. The festivities included church services, picnics, talent shows, and a special service honoring Medgar Evers. There was always a huge outdoor cookout with local and nationally famous entertainers alike. This event brought blacks and whites together with some of the local whites participating.

The biggest event of the homecoming was the party, which could be attended by invitation only, and was always held on the Saturday night of the big weekend. Joe and I were excited to be a part of this event as we got invited every year. If ever there was a time to buy a special outfit, this event would be the time. Partygoers mingled with the rich and famous. We met such greats as B.B. King, Nancy Wilson, Kris Kristofferson, and my favorite, Muhammad Ali, to name a few. We met Anne Rockefeller, daughter of Nelson A. Rockefeller, at one of those affairs. Nelson A. Rockefeller had been appointed vice president after Gerald Ford replaced Richard Nixon as president in 1974.

To outsiders, Joe and I represented progress in Fayette. The mayor introduced us to Ms. Rockefeller and told her, "This is how we live down here in peace and harmony."

Under the Evers administration, Fayette blossomed. The Confederate Memorial Park bustled with black and white shoppers. Business was better than ever. The unemployment rate dropped. The *Fayette Experience* symbolized the changes that had come. It also symbolized the changing attitudes of the white people. Long gone were the television cameras and the *Newsweek* team of reporters. We were settling down to enjoy the fruits of the American dream.

"Elect Charles Evers, the Man Who Cares." That was a saying displayed on one of Mayor Evers's many buttons during his reign as mayor of Fayette. He remained mayor for fifteen years, never fighting exclusively for black rights, but fighting for equal rights for all Jefferson County citizens. Although his office did not give him control over county affairs, his influence and power base did in many ways.

The mayor's goal was to control the economics of the county, control the ballots of the county and the politics. In other words, he wanted to control the entire power structure of counties where blacks were predominant.

Mayor Evers was a massively built man with a spontaneous laugh, who seemed to truly enjoy his power. He always described himself as a loner, one who found it difficult to trust anyone, yet was determined not to let white people teach him how to hate. For those who remembered Mississippi's legendary history of violence and deep-rooted hatred, Charles Evers emerged not only as a determined man, but a heroic one as well.

Mayor Evers was like an evangelical minister; he taught us how to save souls and do battle with the devil. We weren't hollering "Black Power"; we were tasting it firsthand. The black population of Jefferson County believed in the "gospel according to Charles Evers."

Unfortunately, the old maxims of "power corrupts" and "absolute power corrupts absolutely" would only emerge later on.

8
New Start

We had been married two years when we decided to look for a house. By this time, Larry, the store manager, had moved on to open another store, and Joe had been promoted to his position. We knew Fayette was where we planned to live. Joe had long since given up trying to get me to move to California, and I had gotten tired of living in a mobile home, walking back and forth. If Fayette was going to be our home, then we needed more space.

There were not a lot of houses available, as the market for real estate was not that strong. Some new subdivisions were being built in the area, but I wanted an older home, something with character. I wanted a house that I could turn into a home, one with lots of big, spacious rooms. The tract houses were all somewhat alike, cookie-cutter homes with no character, and I didn't like that mold. I knew my instincts would tell me when I found the right one.

It didn't take long. It was an old house with lots of character and charm located about a block off Main Street, nestled between another beautiful, old southern home on the right which also had lots of character, and the only funeral parlor in town on the left. Thick hedges separated the funeral home from the property. The house was built in the 1940s, with big shade trees in the back yard and lots of shrubbery in the front yard. The woman who lived in the house before us loved flowers, and it was surrounded by blooms of many contrasting colors. There was a big sign on the front lawn that read, "Flower Garden of the Month." The yard alone was enough to make me want to see the inside.

On one side of the house was a magnolia tree in full bloom that lent just the right ambiance to the landscape. Awnings were hung over all the windows, which only enhanced the beauty of the old house. Once inside, I fell in love with the twelve-foot ceilings, lots of nooks and crannies, and screened-in front porch. It reminded me a little of the bigger house we'd lived in for a while when I was a child. It was a two-story house with five bedrooms and many other rooms to do with whatever I chose. It even had a butler's pantry. Much repairing and remodeling would be needed to spruce up the inside the way I wanted it, but this house was going to be an exciting challenge for me.

The woman who lived in the other beautiful old southern home next door wasn't too pleased with the possibility of having us as new neighbors. I learned that her name was Mrs. Agnes Ball, and hers was one of the few white families that didn't move out of town when Charles Evers became mayor. She owned a business in town, Ball's Drug Store. The drugstore had been there as far back as I could remember, but I never knew who the owners were.

I suppose Mrs. Ball was really concerned about having us living next door to her because she approached Joe at work one day with a proposition. She told him she had heard that we'd been looking for a house. He confirmed her suspicions, and she proceeded to tell him about another house in a different part of town that we might like. She thought we should take a look at it before we made a final decision. In her opinion, we might be happier living in a more secluded area. Well, that might have been true at one time, but that time had passed.

When Joe came home and very cautiously told me about

the conversation he'd had with Mrs. Ball, I was livid. How could she suggest such a thing? Her intentions were so transparent that even a two-year-old could have seen through her. She also had the nerve to tell him that if we didn't have the money to buy the other house, she would make a loan to us, and we could make arrangements to pay her back. This was just too much for me to swallow, and it was very difficult to keep my cool after hearing how brazen that woman was.

At first, I wanted to go right up to her and give her a piece of my mind. I wanted her to know how I really felt. Instead, after I had calmed down, I called her up and thanked her for the offer. I told her that it was very generous of her to find us a house and offer us a loan to buy it, but we had already decided on the house we wanted to buy. Then I told her, very sweetly, that if she still wanted to buy a house for us, she was free to do so, but we wouldn't be living in it; then I hung the phone up.

Needless to say, after we moved in on November 12, 1976, she remained a very distant neighbor. She did find out, though, that the neighborhood didn't fall apart because we moved in. In fact, we immediately started the renovation process. The first thing I did was have the screened-in porch transformed into a glassed-in porch with heat and air so we could enjoy it all year round. I wasn't too fond of the awnings, so I had those removed, and had a new paint job for the outside of the house as well. We had new shutters put around all the windows in a contrasting color. The house took on a new look but still kept the same old charm.

Shortly after we moved into our new home, I went back to work at New Deal part-time, working two days a week and on holidays and filling in whenever a cashier wanted to go on vacation or just wanted a day off.

We partially furnished the house in the beginning, buying only the necessities. I had fun shopping for just the right pieces of furniture to go with the period of the house. It took us five years to complete the renovations and transform the house into the way we wanted it. I fell in love with my new home and thought I would live there for the rest of my life.

The hurt ran deep whenever Lee promised to come for the children and didn't show up. They waited anxiously by the front door for hours on end. Lee never bothered to call. Sometimes I watched them with sadness as they only left their post long enough to have a bite to eat or go to the bathroom, taking turns so they wouldn't miss his arrival. When night finally came, and they knew he wasn't coming, somehow Nikki always found a way to blame Joe and me. She wouldn't talk to me about the rejection. She just went upstairs to her room, slammed the door, and went to bed with Shea trailing behind her. When I tried talking to her about it, she was silent, pretending to be asleep. I'd sit on the side of her bed, staring into space, and after a while, I gave up, leaving their room in despair.

Nikki told me much later in life that she actually blamed Joe more than she did me. I tried to explain to her that if her father really wanted to see her, then nothing and no one could have kept him away. No matter what the judge had ruled in our divorce decree, I put no limitations on his visits with them. He was always free to visit at will. I did this out of love and concern for my children rather than for Lee's sake.

Joe adopted my children, over Lee's objections, in 1976, two years after we were married. After their adoption, Nikki became more belligerent, if that was possible. She fought against the name change in her own way. I believe she felt that by giving up her father's last name, she would surely lose him for good. She held onto that name for dear life. Whenever she had to write her new name on school papers, she still used her original name. Her teachers tried to explain to her that she was supposed to use her adopted name, but she just wouldn't give in. If the teacher corrected her name on any of her papers, she'd scratch over it and continue to use her old last name.

Joe and I tried to ignore her behavior and hoped, in time, she would learn to accept the adoption. I tried many times to ask her questions to try to discover the root of what was bothering her, but she never gave me a straight answer. She sulked and became very withdrawn. Over the years, we did try counseling, but nothing seemed to help.

I watched my children's behavior for months on end before I decided it was time for us to sit down and try to work through whatever was eating away at them. I told them both that we needed to be very open and honest if we were to get anything resolved. I mostly talked to Nikki as I wasn't sure how much Shea understood. Their feelings toward my marriage to Joe were very important to me. I needed to understand what they were thinking in order for me to help them overcome their fears and concerns. Most of all, I wanted them to know that I loved them and would always be there for them. My marriage to Joe didn't and wouldn't ever change that.

Our conversations became very intense, indeed. They told me things that I never would have suspected, but what I heard sent chills up my spine. Nikki said some of the neighborhood kids said, "Black women have always been whores for white men, so why does your mama think she's any different?" My daughters were told that when Joe got tired of us, he would dump us and move on to some other trusting black woman. They were taunted with, "Then where will you be?" I was very upset and angry when I heard these things. How dare someone say that to my children?

One characteristic children have when they are young is the ability to tell the truth. So it's safe to say that those who taunted Nikki and Shea were repeating what they'd overheard at home. "Your mama is a slut," they were told. "Your mama's a whore." That type of talk was too much coming from elementary-school-age children. When gossip starts to circulate, it has the ability to pervert the truth for those who are on the outside looking in. One's beliefs do not necessarily present the accuracy of any given situation. Nikki grew angrier and angrier about the things she heard. No matter how I tried talking to her, she continued to put up a wall between us. I worried that some day her anger would destroy her more, but I was powerless to do anything about it.

I was totally shocked about what I heard from my daughters, shocked by the racist stereotypes that still existed in the black community. Some speculated that Joe held some threat over my head so that I had to do whatever he said. Some said I was afraid of him for whatever reason. We had all lived through the days, after all, when white men could do whatever they wanted to a black woman with no repercussions.

The concept that "there's no such thing as a black woman being raped or abused" was very much ingrained in the culture. Any man could almost have his way with a black woman and never suffer any consequences. I guess it was hard for some black people to understand that I could actually love a white man and *want* to be with him of my own volition.

Although I was shocked that young children were saying such things to my children, I knew what Nikki and Shea were telling me was reflective of the black community because my integrity was constantly being insulted in public. Black men approached me as if I wore a sign that read, "Free for all." It was almost as if they had the right to insult me. When I didn't respond, I had to hear, "Ain't we good enough for you?"

One day I was in the liquor store next door to New Deal chatting with Carrisa, the cashier who worked behind the counter. A guy I knew who wasn't living in Fayette at the time, but visiting his family there, came in, looked me up and down and asked, "Girl, why in the world did you marry a white man?"

I felt like saying, "None of your business, and get the hell out of my face. The color of a man's skin doesn't make him who he is. Everyone has an opportunity to make choices, and that was my choice!" I had become good at avoiding unpleasant scenes with people, especially men. So instead I laughed and said, "Why, where were you when I was looking for a husband?" I turned and quickly walked out of the store.

As my black community was pulling away from me, I was gradually being welcomed into the family by Joe's relatives. I met Joe's brother Vinnie in 1975. He was working for a car racing company out of California as a turn marshal (someone who aids drivers when their cars flip over, stall, or get stuck). He had been in Atlanta for a race and on his way back home to California he stopped in for a quick visit. My sister Dot made dinner at her house and we all had a good time eating and talking. I never had problems with any of Joe's siblings. Charles, his younger brother, came to visit us often in 1976 after we bought the house.

I met Joe's mom that year too. She was a sweetheart of a lady. She loved having me call her "Mom." I had also met Joe's sisters, Debbie and Jackie. Although I had been to his parents' home more than once, his father, Vincent, was always away at work or out of town on a business trip whenever we were visiting. I don't think we would have gone there at all had he been home.

Once when we were in Connecticut visiting some of Joe's other relatives, we stopped in to see his mom. Joe's family owned their own plane, and his father used to fly from Connecticut to a job he had in New Jersey working at an airport there. We had been at the house a few hours when his father called to say he was on his way home and would be landing in Danbury in about an hour or so. That gave us plenty of time to get up and leave before he got home, and that's just what we did. Joe's father had made it very clear to Joe that he wanted nothing to do with me or Joe's life in Mississippi.

I had met Joe's sister Jackie several times, but we had never spent quality time together until she came to visit us in 1978. We had a good time together—the children included—and while she was there, Joe and I decided to take a short trip and leave her with Nikki and Shea. We thought that would give them a chance to get to know each other without the interference of me being around. The kids were still in school, so Jackie took them to school and picked them up. The schools were integrated by that time, and the school Nikki and Shea went to was predominantly white with only a handful of black kids. Still, Nikki was ashamed to be seen with a white woman. She said the mornings weren't so bad, because the parents all seemed in a hurry to get to their own destinations. The evenings were the worst; no one seemed in a hurry, which gave them more time to take in the situation. She told me each day she wanted to run and hide until everyone had left the school lot where they had to be picked up. She said she walked slowly and as far behind Jackie as she could, hoping no one would see the three of them together.

Shea, two years younger, wasn't as affected by all of this as Nikki was. Shea skipped along, happy to be going home.

Instead of having carefree, fun-filled lives, my children became perpetually concerned about how they would be received by their peers. Most of all, they wondered how to fit in with children their ages. They were normal children growing up in an abnormal household . . . at least by the local standards of that era. Neither of them was very keen on having other kids over to our house. I wish I had encouraged it more so other kids could have seen how we lived a simple life just like any ordinary family.

Joe and I tried to figure out what we could do together to help them get through all of this. So far, he had done little to express his feelings, leaving it up to me to help them deal with our marriage. When I had previously tried to talk to him, he said he didn't really know what to say, because he knew he was being blamed for entering our lives. He said he didn't want them to think that he was trying to take their father's place, because he, too, felt that Lee should be an important presence in their lives. He thought anything he might say this early in the marriage would only create more distance between him and the girls.

Joe came into a ready-made family. I don't think either of us was prepared for the outcome. We knew our marriage was going to affect the children, but we didn't know the depth of those effects. When we saw the pain it caused, neither of us was quite sure how to handle it. My thinking was because the children were so young they would adjust as many children do after a divorce. Instead, I was wrong, and Nikki fought it all the way. I felt helpless, for I was at a complete loss as to how to handle the obstacles that were seemingly taking control of our lives. I felt frustrated, bewildered, and angry at the predicament society had placed on us.

• • •

We had been married five years before I finally met Joe's father in 1979. We had taken a trip to Europe that year, another major source of contention among the townspeople of Fayette. Most black people in Fayette did not travel and the ones that did didn't travel abroad. There were some who felt I had no business traveling to such an exotic place at all. Joe's father asked that we stop in to see them for a few days on our way home. This was a complete turnaround from the man I had heard so much about. I was very apprehensive about this meeting and had many questions as to why he wanted to meet me now after all of these years, but reluctantly I agreed to go along for Joe's sake.

Joe's mother and father picked us up from the airport in New York City. What's so amazing is when I scanned the crowd of waiting people, I picked Joe's father out of that crowd without having ever met him or seen a photo. In the car on our way to his parents' home, his father—Vincent—asked me for a cigarette. I'm not sure how he knew I smoked. I was sitting in back with Joe's mother, Kay, and Joe was sitting up front in the passenger seat with his father. In an accident, years before I met Joe, his father had lost his right hand. My biggest dilemma was trying to decide whether I should light the cigarette for him before I gave it to him. If I didn't, he would have to take his one hand off the wheel to light it himself. Driving from JFK in the traffic was horrendous. I knew if I lit it, I would have to put it between my lips. Would that bother him? I didn't know what to do, so I just took the chance, lit it, passed it to him, and to my surprise, he smoked it without hesitation. I don't think anyone else in the car was aware of what had happened. I couldn't wait until Joe and I were alone so I could tell him what I'd done and what I had been thinking at the time.

When we arrived at the house, Joe's mother showed us to our room. I was still very much overwhelmed by this whole ordeal. We put our bags away, and Joe left me in the room alone to go and talk with his father. I was very relieved to finally be alone so I could think and try to figure out what was supposed to happen next. After putting our things away, I went out to sit and chat for a bit but soon started yawning as the long flight had tired me out.

Thank goodness it was very late when we got in, which I used to my advantage as well, as an excuse to make an immediate exit and not have to continue to try and make small talk. Joe stayed a little longer and talked with his parents, but the long plane ride had worn him out, too. He soon came in to get ready for bed. I was in such a talkative mood that he finally asked me to please shut up so he could get some sleep. I usually fell asleep as soon as my head hit the pillow, but as tired as I was, I couldn't fall asleep. That night there were too many thoughts jumping around in my head. I was still trying to digest that ride from the airport. I remembered seeing Joe's father peering in the rearview mirror, trying to steal glances at me when he thought I wasn't looking.

I was up bright and early the next morning, waking to the smell of bacon frying on the stove. Since I was from the South, Vincent thought that making me a breakfast of grits, eggs, and bacon would make me feel at home. Breakfast was very good, but my stomach was so tense I couldn't eat very much. As soon as I was done, I started having terrible stomach cramps and became terrified that Joe's dad had poisoned me. I asked to be excused from the table and went into the room where Joe and I had slept. Joe followed me, knowing something wasn't quite right. As soon as he closed the door, he asked, "Martha, what's wrong? You look ill."

"Joe," I asked nervously, "are you having any pains in your stomach?"

He answered, "No."

"My God, Joe!" I blurted out. "Your dad has poisoned me!"

He looked at me as if I was crazy, and in some ways, I probably was a little crazy from everything happening so fast. "Martha, what are you talking about?" he said. "My dad wouldn't poison you."

Well, I wasn't so sure at that point, but he did put my fears to rest. I realized that the pain was probably due to the stress I had been under since meeting Joe's dad. When I look back on that incident, it still makes me laugh.

When we returned to Fayette, our daughters, even though they were glad to see us, were still somewhat sullen and belligerent. They felt we had been selfish, going to Europe and leaving them with their Auntie Ruth, even though they loved my sister dearly. It must have seemed to them we were gone much longer than three weeks.

Nikki's influence soon wormed its way into Shea, and she became just as rebellious and as hard to handle, in some ways, as her sister. Some of her actions didn't fit her personality at all. She had always been such an easygoing child. I told her many times just to be herself and stop trying to be like her sister or anyone else, for that matter. My warnings went unheeded.

I had grown up in the same town as my children. The difference was, when I was growing up, we had two worlds, one black and one white. The two occasionally touched or brushed each other, but never met. Now things had changed. The times were different, but many of the feelings were still the same.

During her fourth-grade year, Nikki fully realized her family was different from other families. She said she always knew something was wrong, but couldn't fully put it all together until some of the kids from her school started asking, "Why do you and your sister have a white father?" She said she knew his color was different, but he was not that different looking from her own father, and he wasn't white.

She said that question started her thinking, "Joe is different." She said she came home from school one day and rubbed Joe's skin, but it felt just like hers; the only thing she could see different was the color. Still, she said, she could not understand why her family was treated in such a cold manner because of his skin color.

As Nikki learned more, reality set in and changed both the girls' lives. Shea changed more by what she was taught from Nikki, rather than by what she learned from outside our home. When people stared at us and whispered about us, Nikki knew why. The looks, the whispers, all made sense, but inside, she said, it made her feel very insecure and intimidated. Nikki and Shea told me that those stares we received were what they began to hate the most. They said they felt as if they were living two lives, one in the black world and a different one in the white world.

Both girls told me that, although they knew how white people felt about us, it was different when the prejudice came from black people. They said it was twice as bad. They said some of the kids they played with called them names such as *zebras*, *newspapers*, and *Oreos*—anything having a black-and-white connotation.

Nikki said she used to ask herself, "Why did our mom have to marry a white man?" The attention we all received when we were out together as a family was sometimes unbearable, which made them both feel resentful. Nikki said it was much better if it was just the three of us, alone, because we didn't draw any particular attention; we just blended in with the crowd.

I experienced all sorts of feelings toward my ex-husband, but mostly anger over his not being more supportive of Nikki and Shea. The few times I did manage to encourage him to take the kids for a visit, he'd take them to his parents' house, drop them off, and leave. His mother then fueled them with lies about me and my marriage. In all fairness, I have to say that Lee's father wasn't mean to me, and he didn't talk about me to the girls. He took them fishing at the pond near their house and let them run and play as two little kids should be able to do. He tried to be a good grandparent.

Rather than try to help me explain our life, such as it was, Lee helped make it worse by redoubling his efforts to repeat gossip to the children and encouraging his mother to do the same. He repeatedly told Nikki and Shea that Joe broke up our family, and Joe was the reason he didn't come around to see them. Rather than taking responsibility for his drinking, his affairs, his abuse, Lee heaped the blame on Joe and me. His mother didn't know the meaning of restraining her mouth for the sake of the children. I became so fed up with their maliciousness that when Lee didn't initiate any contact with the girls, I didn't initiate it either. Their visits with Lee and his family proved to be more destructive than positive. I had to finally cut them off completely.

Gradually, however, the tensions eased somewhat and we developed a mixed circle of friends. I met new people, both black and white, mostly through the grocery business. I knew the previous owner, his wife, and several of his family members. We became friends with the lawyer who had handled my divorce, Frank Walden, and his wife, Beverly, and with our insurance agent and his wife. We got to know Dr.

Humphrey and his wife. They were black and we got really close with them. Joe also became more and more involved in the Fayette business community. He joined the chamber of commerce, which at the time was about 30 percent white, 70 percent black. All of this made me feel that we had established ourselves in the community, and in a larger more diverse community than the one I had grown up in. We had settled in, going on with our lives.

An Eagle Scout himself, Joe became the scoutmaster for the local Boy Scout troop, which was all black, and he raised funds in the community that enabled him to give the scouts experiences that no one had ever given those boys in Fayette before. We took them to Disney World in Florida, the big WWII Aircraft Center, "The Yorktown," in Charleston, South Carolina, and the National Jamboree that was held every four years in Virginia, where the boys met the First Lady, Nancy Reagan. There were also backpacking trips to New Mexico, Colorado, North Carolina, and other places.

Joe's growing involvement brought more new friends into our lives, like Cal Brownstone, a black Fayette policeman, who also helped raise funds for the Boy Scout troop. Joe had met Cal during Mayor Evers's gubernatorial campaign, and they had been involved in many community activities together.

Cal loved collard greens and cornbread, so whenever I made that for dinner I'd call and tell him and he'd come over, most of the time while on duty . . . or stop by for a cup of coffee if he was working the late shift. He'd eat, chat with us, and then get back on the job. Cal was a great conversationalist with strong opinions on most subjects, which made him an intriguing person to talk to. He became a good friend.

The more well known Joe became in the community at large, the more we felt accepted. At times, however, Joe's growing prominence rubbed our mayor the wrong way. There was only room for one kingpin in Fayette, and Mayor Evers wanted to make sure he was it. When he felt Joe was getting too big for his britches or he got irritated with Joe about something Joe had done, he would retaliate in subtle ways, like slowing down the garbage pickup at the store, or raising the price for garbage pickup. When Joe complained, Mr. Evers always told him that it was *just politics*. No matter what the situation was, he stuck with that old phrase: "It's politics; nothing personal." Even with a few minor run-ins, however, Joe maintained a cordial relationship with Mayor Evers. No one wanted to be on Charles Evers's bad side.

When Mayor Evers asked Joe to hire Cal Brownstone in his off hours as a part-time stock clerk at New Deal, it was an easy request to fulfill because Joe liked Cal and felt having the presence of a policeman on the premises would help curtail theft. But he also did it because in Fayette you did what the mayor wanted.

"Joe is really happy to have you aboard," I told Cal one night when he was leaving our house.

"Well, I'm, glad," he said jocularly, "because if I'm ever fired from New Deal, there will be hell to pay!"

I laughed, and he laughed.

When he said the same thing to me another time . . . and then still another time, I was baffled by his need to repeat the joke. When I told Joe, he shrugged the comment off. "Fired? I'd hate to lose him," Joe said, "He's so fun-loving and mischievous, the customers are really drawn to him." Joe chuckled. "Cal's been known to put a bar of soap in customers' carts without their being aware of it if he thinks they need it."

Neither of us took the remark as a threat, but I didn't entirely forget his words. I sort of tucked them away in the back of my mind.

It was a good time. We were comfortable in the community and the girls had become more comfortable with their lives, and we began living more like a real family. Shea warmed up to Joe. Nikki, too wasn't quite as standoffish as she had been and became distracted by her interest in sports—baseball, track, and even though she was too short, she still tried out for the basketball team.

Everything was finally progressing. I was very much into the busy schedule of my children's lives with school and all the activities. Life felt good again; we were finally able to breathe a sigh of relief . . . an all-too-brief sigh of relief.

9
The Boycott

The New Deal Supermarket was Fayette's pride and joy. Up until 1973, Fayette only had small mom-and-pop grocery stores, and if you wanted to shop at a supermarket, you had to drive twenty-five miles to Natchez. Having the convenience of shopping in town made the New Deal very popular. It was professionally run, and a financial success, but it also had a personal touch. If a customer wanted a particular item that wasn't in stock, management ordered it for the patron. In a sense, the New Deal was a symbol of the way things in Fayette were going in 1979. The town had been steadily moving ahead over the years. People, both blacks and whites, were beginning to relax more and learn how to enjoy all that we had fought so hard to achieve.

Then weird things started happening. About a month after Joe hired Cal Brownstone, we started hearing rumors from employees that an effort was afoot to undermine the store financially. We were told that two of our cashiers were charging customers less than they should, and the idea for doing so was Cal Brownstone's.

One day, soon after these rumors started, I was working at the first register (there were four registers in all) and one of the cashiers in question was working the second register right near me. I could plainly see what was going on, and I could tell that the final receipt was much too short to include all the items the customer had bought.

Joe and I then asked a very trustworthy lady we both knew

well to come in and shop just to see if she could get away with paying less for more merchandise. We told her to go through one of the two lines the cashiers we'd heard about worked. She did. She showed Joe both the bagged groceries she'd bought and the receipt for what she'd paid, and the two didn't match.

On the days the two cashiers worked, the store was losing thousands of dollars.

Joe confronted one of the cashiers and she denied it at first, but then came clean about the whole scheme. She even admitted that she and the other cashier had been planted in the store just for that reason. In addition, she told Joe who was behind this operation: *Cal Brownstone.*

Joe fired the two cashiers and told Rayvon Smith, New Deal's owner, and he fired Cal. "You can't prove a thing," Cal told him, and in a way he was right. There was no proof he had anything to do with those cashiers; it was just their word against his, but they both took polygraph tests, and he refused to.

The last words Cal uttered as he walked out of the store that evening were, "You'll be sorry for this; just you wait and see."

Joe and I were really hurt, because we thought we had a solid, close relationship with Cal. We couldn't figure out why he'd do such a thing. He was very close to Mayor Evers, however, and we wondered whether this was another way for the mayor to take Joe down a peg. Was this, too, "nothing personal, just politics"?

The next thing we knew there was another rumor: the store was going to be boycotted. I asked Cal about the rumor, and he pretended he knew nothing, but gave me a look that said, "Don't say I didn't warn you."

Figure 5. Boycotters at New Deal Supermarket

And then, sure enough, on Friday, January 11, 1979, two days after Cal was fired, all hell broke loose. Joe went in to work early, as always, and did the usual things in preparation for opening up shop. The other employees came to work, punched their time cards, and got ready to start their work day. Around 8:00 a.m. he went to unlock the door for business, and that's when he noticed people outside the store with picket signs. He called me and said maybe I shouldn't come in to work that morning, and when I asked why, he said because the store was being boycotted. I got up, got dressed, and drove by the store to see for myself.

What I saw was absolutely shocking. It was cold and damp that morning with a mist of fine rain. There were men set up at all three entrances to the Fayette Plaza's parking lot walking around with signs hanging from around their necks. They all had on coats and gloves with hats pulled down over their ears to help keep them warm. The blacks who attempted to enter the parking lot area, whether they were going to the store or some other business in the plaza, were harassed verbally, and in some instances, physically. The boycott not only hurt New Deal, but the other businesses in the shopping plaza as well. The group of boycotters with their signs didn't try to find out what business the customer was going to patronize in the plaza. They just warned all the people to stay away, stopping all cars and anyone entering the plaza on foot.

A college student from Alcorn State University (ASU) came to the liquor store, seemingly unaware of what was going on. The college was at least twenty miles from Fayette and whatever went on in town rarely had any effect on the campus. As the young man exited his car to enter the liquor store, he was warned not to go in. He ignored the warning and went in anyway. He purchased the bottle of his choice and started back to his car. As he was trying to get in, he was grabbed and pushed to the ground, and his purchase was taken from him and smashed to the ground. After a few punches along with lots of threats, he was put into his car and told to leave but not before being told what would happen if he came back. The young man called the store and told Joe what had happened. Joe called the police to report the incident, but no one from the department ever showed up to investigate the story.

So far no one from the police department had come to see what was going on. They did not cooperate at all in protecting the customers. That might be because one member of the department was organizing the boycott. From the very beginning, the boycotters were meeting at the police station, making their signs, and being driven to the store's parking lot in police cars, one of which was driven by Captain Cal Brownstone fully dressed in his uniform. Cal also brought his picketers food during lunchtime and paid them to participate. It was obvious that he was able to pull off the boycott successfully because he had the backing not only of the police department, but also of the mayor.

Nothing happened in Fayette, Mississippi, at that time without the knowledge and backing of Mayor Evers, and this was a major happening. New Deal owner Rayvon Smith called the mayor. Many concerned citizens called the mayor, asking him to intervene before the boycott got out of hand, but the mayor had stayed away, stating that he had nothing to do with the boycott. He said, "I'm neutral." The boycott, he insisted, was between Joe and Cal, and only they could work it out.

Ironically, Fayette was the first Mississippi town to have a black mayor, the town where most of the population and most of the elected officials were black, and this was a boycott that was pitting blacks against blacks. All of the picketers were black and all of the people being prevented from shopping were black. It was a return to the old segregationist policy of "whites only" because the picketers actually let whites through the line to shop. Indeed, many of the white customers commented on how nice it was to shop without having to fight the crowds or drive around looking for a parking space. Most said that since it didn't affect them, there was no reason for them to involve themselves.

The actual motive for the mayor taking a "neutral" stand was a mystery. The only logical reason anyone could come up with was that it was his town, and he could do as he damn well pleased. I believe he had developed some sort of jealousy or resentment toward Joe, and thought the boycott would be a small incident ("nothing personal, just politics") that would make a statement and pass. However, it got out of control.

Who was financing the boycott? It was reported in our local newspaper that Cal had purchased twenty sheets of poster board with a $100 bill the morning of the boycott from the *Fayette Chronicle*. Most of those walking the picket line were the town winos. The newspaper also reported that when one was asked why he was out there walking a picket line, he said, "Man, I get paid thirty bucks for every shift I walk." He would not say by whom. Others stated the boycotters were paid in liquor.

Just who was Cal Brownstone? No one really knew the answer to that question. Joe and I read in the paper that there were federal agents in town investigating charges that were filed against him dating back to 1965. According to one report, Cal was working as a door guard at a Chicago nightclub when he shot and killed a man in a fight at the bar. The mayor said, even though Cal was a convicted felon, he still was a good policeman, and that what happened in the past had nothing to do with what was going on now.

The store remained open during the time of the boycott, but took in only a fraction of the revenues it should have. A few of the employees came to work every day and waited on the few white customers who came in, but most of the employees had to be laid off.

Four days into the boycott, Joe and I started receiving threatening phone calls about our safety. Taking precautions, we were escorted to and from our home by employees and family members. They showed their concern by standing guard, unasked, at our home and at the store. Some of them took turns watching our children, as well. It was no longer safe to park our cars in back of the store. We began to live in fear.

I was sick and tired of waiting to see what was going to happen next, sick and tired of cautionary doubts. Someone had to take some kind of action. Joe and I began calling upon friends to call anyone they knew who might be tired of sitting back and allowing a few people to take over their rights. From that, we had enough people to organize a group that we named the Committee for Freedom of Choice.

Dorothy Humphrey, my former teacher and a good friend of ours, was instrumental in helping me organize the committee. She and I called everyone we could, using the telephone directory, telling them what we were planning and asking for their help and support. We explained to them that we wanted to have a walk-in that Monday morning in an attempt to break the boycott. The fliers read:

> Take a stand!
> If you want the right to enter and shop at New Deal, meet with the concerned citizens at 4:30 p. m. January 15th at the field in front of Lehmann Auto Company. We plan to go as a unified group all at the same time. We have notified the Fayette Police Department, the Sheriff's Department, as well as the Mississippi Highway Patrol, in the hopes that no one will be harmed.
> Tell your friends and relatives to help support the future of their community and their freedom.

A group of more than three hundred irate supporters showed up that Monday morning to break the boycott. We all got in our cars and drove in a single line to New Deal Shopping Center. We marched in as a unified group, without talking or responding to any of the boycotters or news media hanging around to ask questions. This was to be a silent walk-in. Defying the boycott had become a moral issue for the entire town.

When we got out of our cars and started to walk in, the boycotters all huddled together on one side of the parking lot, staring viciously, but afraid to try anything because of the presence of the press.

The police chief arrived, for the first time since this all started, with members of his force. He told the reporters that he had been sent there by the mayor to keep the peace. Everyone there knew that wasn't true; he had been sent there to observe and report back to the mayor.

As the walk-in ended and the people were leaving to go home, the press honed in on them. Reporters and photographers sent from Natchez and Jackson swarmed the plaza, rolling television cameras, snapping pictures, and talking to anyone who would take the time to answer questions.

Cal Brownstone was there on the edge of the parking lot, standing with his attorney, refusing to talk with any news media or answer any questions concerning the boycott. Mr. Smith did tell the press that he would file an injunction against the marchers if any more instances of violence occurred around his store.

The next day all the local television stations carried the story of the walk-in. It made the headlines in neighboring newspapers the *Natchez Democrat* and the *Jackson Daily News*, as well as the local one, the *Fayette Chronicle*.

On Wednesday morning after the big walk-in protest of the boycott, people came in and resumed shopping for about an hour. Most of the customers thought they were going to be able to do business as usual. However, at 9:00 a.m., the marchers were back at their posts, blocking the entrance to the store with more verbal abuse and threats.

The boycotters were still meeting at the police station, making their signs, and being driven to the store in police cars. There were about twelve of them, six more than when they started. Their intimidating looks were enough to frighten some of the people and keep them away, especially the older folks. People didn't readily take to the streets and become demonstrators. In Fayette, the sight of black demonstrators was very rare indeed.

Cal was never relieved of his duties as a policeman, which by all accounts was a conflict of interest. All through this, the mayor maintained his innocence of any wrongdoing. Whenever confronted, he said this boycott grew out of a personal dispute between three disgruntled employees and Joe. It had nothing to do with him. He also stated that a city policeman certainly had the right to boycott just as anyone else did, so long as it was done peacefully.

New Deal was the largest volume business in Fayette, providing the city with a large portion of its sales tax. To close the doors would have hurt us personally, but it would have also hurt the whole town. Many attempts had been made to end the dispute, but the attorneys on both sides could not reach an agreement acceptable to the owner, Mr. Smith, or to Cal Brownstone.

Thursday morning around 4:00 a.m., the town awoke to what seemed like a towering inferno. The smoke was so thick it looked like the whole town was on fire. The old Guilminot Hotel building, the last historic landmark in town, which was also owned by Mr. Smith, burned to the ground in the predawn hours. The sheriff's department called in the state troopers, because the situation had gotten completely out of control. Sheriff J. P. Wallace suspected that the blaze was a direct result of arson, but it was never proven who caused it. He called in a fire marshal from Jackson to investigate, and his suspicions of arson were confirmed.

Several people, who had been awake at that hour getting ready for work, reported that shortly after 4:00 a.m., they had heard a sound, which was something like a firecracker or a small explosion of some kind, but didn't think much of it at the time.

The fire was reported at 4:15 that morning, but it was nearly an hour later before the fire whistle was blown. Some observers said that as they watched the fire, the top and bottom floors were burning first. It was a sight to be seen. One onlooker said the fire resembled the burning of Atlanta during the Civil War as was depicted in *Gone with the Wind*. A reporter from one of the daily newspapers stated that when he checked in at the police department that morning, there was no record of a fire having been reported at all.

The Natchez, Port Gibson, and Vicksburg Fire Departments were called in to assist the Fayette Fire Department in fighting the blaze. It was the opinion of the people viewing the fire that if it had not been for a foggy night with a light rain and, fortunately, no wind, most of our little town would have burned down. The picture at dawn that morning was the shell of the burned-out hotel building and smoldering debris all along the streets.

The building, although it had been unoccupied for over a month, was valued at more than $100,000. It was being used for office space, but due to renovations that were to begin that same week, all of the previous tenants had moved out.

Other businesses that were close to the fire had to be hosed down. Several windows were blown out of some of the buildings across the street from the hotel. The fire also damaged cable and telephone lines, which caused an interruption of service for some of the merchants.

The image of that morning, the vision of the damage and the smoke covering the town, was etched in the minds of the people. The town was immobilized by fear. It seemed as if the boycott was getting much too hostile and much too dangerous. Something had to be done, and soon, before someone got seriously injured.

Since it followed the aftermath of the walk-in, some believed that it was done in retaliation for the shoppers crossing the picket line. The marchers were back at their posts, one carrying a sign that read, "New Deal will burn next."

We began getting threatening phone calls.

"Hello."
"Your house will be next to be burned." Click.

"Hello."
"If we see your car on the back parking lot, it will be destroyed."

"Hello."
"You'd better watch your back."

The fire smoked and burned for days and sparked a mad rush to buy weapons. The people felt that if they couldn't receive protection from the town's policemen, then they were going to have to defend themselves. The Thursday after the fire at 5:00 p.m., the manager of the local Western Auto reported that he had sold out of firearms and ammunition. The sheriff's department let it be known that if the people didn't receive proper protection, then they would be forced to ask the state for help. Some of the residents began to wear guns as an atmosphere of fear settled over the town. The general feeling was that the boycott would not stop until someone got hurt.

Sheriff J. P. Wallace called in state troopers to assist him, keeping other law officials on a standby basis. They were stationed at the store and at our home, around the clock. I gave up trying to go anywhere, because I was being harassed and followed by some of Cal's supporters, which made the boycott seem somewhat personal.

The fire only seemed to recharge the marchers, because early Friday morning, they were back at the store with renewed threats of burning down the homes of anyone who crossed the picket line. They harassed any customer who tried to gain entrance into any of the businesses. They told customers that their tires would be slashed if they left their cars in the parking lot unattended.

Meanwhile, unopened stock in the supermarket was being loaded onto a truck to be moved out. Mr. Smith didn't want to close the store, but with no support from the mayor, he was left with little choice. The store's business had drastically dropped during the past week. Most customers refused to cross the picket line because they were afraid for their safety and that of their families. It was reported in the newspaper that Joe said, "Our business is zilch."

Every attempt to end the dispute had failed. The mayor, according to his spokesperson, was out of town, and he could not be reached for comment. Things looked very grim. Attorneys for both sides had tried several times, unsuccessfully, to put an end to the boycott, but they were deadlocked on any kind of settlement. Mr. Smith agreed to reconsider hiring two of the employees back, but there was no way he would consider rehiring Cal Brownstone. He said, "The two cashiers had not been officially charged with any wrongdoing; they were dismissed based on the results from the polygraph tests administered."

Word spread fast that New Deal was closing its doors. The people driving by noticed the big grocery trucks backed up, loading boxes onto flatbeds. That was a devastating sight to the citizens in the community. It looked as if they were about to lose the only grocery store in town.

The day after the fire, a group of approximately five hundred irate citizens demanded that the mayor and board of aldermen settle this boycott before any more violence or vandalism occurred. They demanded that a meeting be held that very day.

With the state highway patrol and county sheriff's officers standing guard around town, the residents of Fayette overwhelmingly approached the mayor and his board of aldermen to endorse some kind of amicable compromise that would satisfy both parties so that all of our lives could get back to normal.

Although the mayor maintained he was not involved, he did call an emergency meeting to be held at the courthouse for 7:00 p.m. that evening. During the meeting, speakers were cheered and booed by a predominantly black crowd. The majority of the crowd demanded that something be done immediately to settle this boycott once and for all. They stated that they would not be leaving until the situation was resolved. The scene in the packed courtroom was chaotic with people spilling out into the hallways.

Mayor Evers promised to meet with Mr. Smith and Joe right after the meeting to see if they would accept the compromise that had been put before them. He wanted the two female employees rehired and Cal to take his grievances through the legal channel of the courts. That's what most people thought should have happened all along. The two women declined to return to work but did get a month's severance pay.

After that meeting, it was reported that the mayor called an executive session at his office with the board of aldermen and the police chief. Cal agreed to lift the boycott after he re-

Figure 6. Remains of the Guilminot Hotel after the fire

ceived a month's severance pay from New Deal as well. The very next day, the boycott was lifted. Later that night, Cal, his attorney, and the mayor came by the store. They stood outside for a long time, talking in quiet tones. Obviously, their purpose was intimidation, for that was the prevailing theme throughout the boycott.

The boycott, combined with the burning of the old hotel, was a turning point in the mayor's career; it was the catalyst that turned our quiet town upside down. Although the boycott had ended and the compromises were met, the bad memories lingered on for a long time. No one at the time quite understood the long-range consequences of that boycott.

The smoking hulk of the Guilminot Hotel still brooded over downtown. Three stately walls and a pile of bricks were all that remained of one of Fayette's oldest historical buildings. While a crew began knocking down what remained of the hotel, townspeople looked up at the empty facade looming over Main Street like a movie set and remembered the building's hundred-year-old history.

All in all, there was an unsettling sadness about the boycott. Too much violence was perpetuated and carried out verbally as well as physically. It was too intense and far too personal. To pit blacks against blacks was a setback for our community. The mayor's inexcusable negligence caused the townspeople to think deeper. Would he sit back and allow other situations to get out of control the way he had let the boycott get out of control, before stepping in? We had not elected the mayor to represent *some* of the people, but *all* of the people. The town needed a mayor who would be unbiased in personal disputes among the citizens in the community.

Kennie Middleton, an attorney in Fayette, said it best: "To say that the mayor was neutral, in regard to the boycott, would be like saying that Ayatollah Khomeini was neutral in regard to the holding of the American hostages in Iran!"

By 1981, Charles Evers had been mayor for three terms. That March, he announced his plans to run for a fourth term. He stressed to the community the accomplishments under his administration during the past twelve years. He also spoke about pending projects, which were either under way or being planned. He said that he was currently negotiating with such federal agencies as FHA to obtain funds for a new water system for our town. Mayor Evers indicated that the amount of money involved was approximately $2 million for the water project alone.

Concerned citizens asked Kennie Middleton to run against Evers. The same week the mayor announced his plans for re-election, Kennie Middleton also announced his plans to run against him.

Kennie was a prominent attorney practicing law in Fay-

Figure 7. Kennie Middleton

ette. He was a local who had gone away to pursue his education, graduating from Southern University in Baton Rouge, Louisiana, in 1972, and then graduating from the University of Mississippi in Oxford, Mississippi, with a law degree in '74. After spending a few years there, he and his wife, Claudine, decided to return home. His slogan was, "We have seen what Fayette can do for one man; now let's see what one man can do for Fayette."

There was a feeling that there had been a bit of cronyism going on in Fayette—greedy hands belonging to those close to power taking more from the pot for themselves and distributing the leftovers to others. Kennie was very much aware of the town's problems as far as its economic survival was concerned. He knew our elected officials had to possess the knowledge and capabilities necessary to assure the greatest possible number of people a means of making a living, not just a selected few. Usually small town politics are handled a little differently from larger towns or cities. It seemed in our town greedy hands took more from the pot and distributed what was left.

In his reelection campaign, the mayor said, "This community has come a long way, and my reason for offering my continued service to the people of our fair city is to make sure that the upward and progressive movement of our community is not disrupted but maintained." He told the people to look back at what he had done and let his work speak for him.

During Evers's tenure, our town had grown increasingly dependent upon federal funding. Yet, even with those funds, our unemployment rate was steadily rising, while the population was rapidly decreasing. Many people had expressed concerns about the direction the town seemed to be heading. Many were even torn about how much loyalty they should extend to the mayor.

During the first three years of the Evers administration, the mayor had attracted more than $10 million dollars to Fayette, both in federal and private funding, including a new garbage truck New York City sold the town for $1.00. The effects of his efforts were dramatic. However, statistics did suggest that the progress he had brought into the town was not permanent. Unemployment stalled at 18 percent in the last eight years of the mayor's leadership. Young people could not find local work, in either Fayette or in nearby Natchez. They spent most of their days idly lurking under the big shade trees along Main Street.

In 1982, when Kennie Middleton defeated him for mayor, Evers was quoted as saying, "I lost because I didn't campaign hard enough." The truth was, in the past, he had hardly campaigned at all, because he never before had a viable candidate running against him. This time he not only had competition; his accomplishments for the town were old news, and he had a dark smudge on his record, thanks to Cal Brown-stone. The handling of the boycott simply brought back too many memories and unsettling thoughts about years past when we still lived in fear under the white man's law. Living through the turmoil of the boycott and the burning of the old hotel was like the opening of an old wound for the entire community.

After the election, when people were looking for the new mayor, they were directed around the corner from city hall to Kennie E. Middleton's storefront law office on Main Street. In the beginning, there was a lot of friction between the former mayor and the newly elected one. Evers accused Middleton of misusing funds, using city property for personal use, and many other petty things. Basically, he criticized everything the new administration did or didn't do. He was a sore loser. Were the accusations true? I can't say with certainty that they were true or false, but the general opinion was that the old mayor was grasping at straws, trying to make the present administration look incompetent. Evers knew that, while Kennie was an excellent attorney, he didn't have the national connections he had and he used that knowledge to his advantage whenever it suited him.

Still, filling the charismatic Evers's shoes was not easy. When trying to follow a dynamic personality, one always finds difficulties. Charles Evers was a combination of what he had to be for the time and what we, the people, made him. He had always called the shots, and if anyone crossed him there was always a price to pay. That's not to say everything he did was bad.

I had to admit that the years of the Evers administration had been some of the most amazing years of my life. The involvement, the commitment, and the changes had been unbelievable. Now the town needed to keep moving, but in another direction.

The town was buzzing again; this time, over the shock of the outcome of the election. Although some citizens had expressed their desire for a change, I don't think they thought it would actually happen. I believe both mayors were good for the town, but they were as divided in their approaches to creating prosperity in Fayette as they were in their personal styles of management and their philosophies of leadership.

Mayor Evers forced changes under his leadership, while Mayor Middleton was trained for changes that already existed. The townspeople decided to forgo the heavy-handed and flamboyant Evers influence they had chosen for the past twelve years, in favor of a man who was thoughtful, considerate, and religious.

Our new mayor took office and tried to repair the damage that had been done by the previous administration. He saw the need to improve the quality of life in Fayette for the broad spectrum of the town's citizens. Mayor Middleton was not an opponent of Evers as much as he was a proponent of further progress.

In 1980, Joe and I became storeowners. We bought New Deal Supermarket from Rayvon Smith, which extended a bigger commitment on our part to our little community. We thought we could finally relax. We felt we had proven ourselves to be part of the community at last.

10
The Election

In the spring of 1983, our local paper, the *Fayette Chronicle*, announced that Joe Rossignol of Fayette had decided to run for supervisor of District 3, Jefferson County.

This was the first time Joe had ever run for political office, but it came at the end of many years of his very active involvement in the Fayette community. By this time he'd been part of the New Deal Supermarket—as manager and then owner—for almost a decade, and he strongly believed that if a community supports your business, you have to give back to the community. As one of only three whites on the twelve-member Board of the Jefferson County Chamber of Commerce, he had served as both vice president and secretary/treasurer and worked hard to achieve "key community" status for Fayette from the state government. This made Fayette a prime candidate for getting companies to invest in businesses and factories in the area.

He was vice chairman of the Jefferson County Democratic Party, and had been involved in local democratic politics as long as he'd been in Mississippi. The governor had appointed him to the State Job Training Coordinating Council in 1984, and he was a member of the Executive Committee of the County Welfare Board.

He was perhaps best known for—and proudest of—what he'd done for his young Boy Scouts, for Troop 287. While most Boy Scout troops had about twenty-five members, Joe and his co–Scout leader, Mr. Ballard, the junior high principal, had over a hundred Boy Scouts, most of whom had never been outside Mississippi and who couldn't afford Boy Scout uniforms. They provided uniforms through donations from other businesses, went on one hike per month, camped out three or four times a year and took the boys on at least one travel activity per month—exposing them to places like New Orleans, Houston, Washington, DC, the Phil Mont scout ranch in New Mexico, Joyce Kilmer Wilderness Area in North Carolina, and Crested Butte, Colorado. Every year they sent a dozen Boy Scouts to summer camp for one week at Camp Kickapoo. Using raffle tickets, the scouts raised half the money for all these activities, and Joe and local business owners paid the balance.

Their troop was one of the few black troops at state and national jamborees. They slept in large tents donated by the ROTC. White Scoutmasters from their district were always cordial but full of questions of how they managed so many boys, while other Scoutmasters only had a dozen in each of their camp sites. Even though they were an oddity in the size of their members and their color, they earned the respect of other troops, winning their share of competitions at Boy Scout events (and always taking first place in any event that involved sports or running). Joe was very proud of his Scouts, and received awards for what he'd done and appreciation from the community as a whole.

Running for office felt like something whose time had come. During the past decade, Joe had a proven record of commitment, experience, and dedication. He had also proven to be results-driven. Action was what we needed, and he had definitely proven himself to be a man of action. He wanted to show the community that he could use his organizational abilities to do for them what he had done for the Scouts.

Joe's campaign was unique to the area in that he proposed to break with political traditions and present a well-thought-out platform of ideas to modernize the county government. He recognized the need to close the gap between the city and county and to create a more productive working relationship between the elected officials and the businessmen to assure maximum use of public and private resources. He felt Jefferson County needed good leadership, community pride, and a cooperative spirit to continue to move forward, and he could help build that.

In his campaign, Joe pointed out that no one would have guessed, looking around locally, that Mississippi ranked first in road expenditures. The roads of Jefferson County were roads of inefficiency, of poor management, of wasted resources, of worn-out methods—in other words, roads were just plain falling apart.

Joe's thoughts were that running for supervisor of his district would enable him to do more for the community. In doing for the community, it would be a way to show his appreciation for the support we had received during the turbulent days of the boycott. He felt being a successful businessman gave him the background knowledge he needed to help plan the future of our county government. His reputation and experience had shown he would serve the people without regard to race, sex, or religion.

Fayette was buzzing with gossip, this time political gossip: who's running against whom, who's running for what position? Thanks to Mayor Evers's influence, by now there weren't very many people who were not registered voters, but the issue was getting those who had registered out to vote on Election Day.

That year we seemed to have more candidates than necessary for the positions. There were seventeen positions to be filled and forty-seven candidates running to fill them. Of the forty-seven, thirty were black. Politics often divides people in small communities. It certainly seemed to have put an uncomfortable, fractious edge in the air, almost like having a big war in a small country with tempers flying around like bullets.

That might have just been my interpretation. Personally, I didn't want to have anything to do with politics, because I was more of an introvert than an extrovert. I'd always cherished my privacy, and becoming involved in the political world made me feel that a certain amount of my privacy was about to be lost. But when Joe made up his mind that he wanted to run for the position, I felt that the least I could do was support him. With his experience, he truly believed he was the best man for the job and so did I.

Joe and I had heard talk that someone famous might be coming into town to help motivate the people to go to the polls. It turned out to be the great Reverend Jesse Jackson, director of People United to Save Humanity (PUSH), an organization devoted to gaining economic power for blacks.

Jackson was an idol to the blacks in our town, including me, someone whom the people of Jefferson County believed in. For him to take the time out of his busy schedule to visit and talk with us was something to be excited about. And we were excited.

I, along with everyone else, was delighted for the opportunity to meet the famous Rev. Jesse Jackson. Having no idea what an impact his presence would have on my life, I was anticipating his visit with the utmost respect. I had read and heard about his achievements and couldn't wait to see him in person.

On Monday, August 10, 1983, I left home early to get a good spot on the crowded street in front of the courthouse so that I could see Rev. Jackson close up and hear his speech. As the crowd anxiously awaited the entrance of the guest speaker, the mayor stepped forward to give the introductions, and then lo and behold: on the courthouse steps in Fayette, Mississippi, the mighty Rev. Jesse Jackson came out and led us in prayer. He then told the crowd of about 500 that there was evidence of change in our great state. He pointed out that in May of 1983, more than 40,000 blacks who previously had not been registered were now registered voters. In June of 1983, another 1,600 blacks were registered in the state of Mississippi alone.

County elections in seventeen counties had been held up due to court intervention over redistricting, and 300 observers were scheduled to be on hand for those elections. He told the excited crowd that it was because of those facts that this election would be emancipation day for blacks throughout Mississippi. He said that when blacks took over the leadership of our state, the power would shift. "When we get through on Tuesday, voting day," he told the crowd, "Mississippi will never be the same again."

He held up his hand to halt the noise and then asked the crowd, "Is there anyone in the audience today who is not registered to vote, and if so, please step forward now."

Four young people came forward, and they were immediately escorted to the circuit court's office to register.

Rev. Jackson urged the people to vote before they went to work on the morning of the election; otherwise, he said, they might not be allowed time off to go to the polls in the evenings. "If we the people vote right on Tuesday," he shouted to the crowd, "come Wednesday morning, we will all be our own bosses!"

The already-wired crowd became even more pumped up

after those powerful words. They absorbed his every phrase as if they were sponges. He had everyone's attention by then.

He told us we didn't need more jobs, we needed more positions of power. We should be able to collect the taxes and distribute the money. Then he ran through a long list of Mississippi's political offices and pointed out the disparaging number of blacks versus whites who held those positions. "Our time has come!" he told the crowd.

He was mesmerizing. I was just as entranced as the people around me; I believed in that man. He had such a powerful and trustworthy tone to his voice. Toward the end of each sentence of his speech, there was a hint of the flavor of a Southern Baptist minister. He told us we were not asking for welfare; we were asking for *our share*.

Everything he said, I had been in agreement with. We *did* need more black leadership in Mississippi. Fayette had been the start of so many changes during the turbulent civil rights years; why not continue in our leadership? "It's time for a change!" stated Rev. Jackson.

"YES!" I cheered.

But then the bubble burst. Jesse Jackson was asked to read off the names of the candidates who were running on Tuesday, August 11. He read each candidate's name and then paused to give the crowd ample time to applaud.

Joe was standing right behind Jackson and was able to look over his shoulder to read the note that was handed to Rev. Jackson before he had a chance to read it to the crowd. That enabled Joe to prepare himself for what we were to hear next.

Joe said his biggest dilemma was how to react to the statement. He said his initial feeling was to shout out something clever to the crowd. However, his better judgment made him realize that the most important thing to the people on that hot, August day was having the great Jesse Jackson in town. For that reason he silently stood by as he heard Rev. Jackson say, when he got to Joe's name on the ballot: "On my paper, it says here, 'Uncle Joe is a definite no-no.'"

I had spent ninety minutes standing in the extreme heat with the sun pouring down on my back for this? I had rushed to get up close enough to see and hear my hero, only to have him vilify my husband?

I could not believe Jesse Jackson would say such a thing, could not believe I had heard correctly. I wanted to say, "Would you repeat that last sentence, please?" but the silence around me confirmed what I thought I had heard. The crowd seemed just as shocked as I was. For the first time in his speech, he'd made a statement that received no applause. The crowd got really quiet, so quiet you could have heard a pin drop.

Uncle Joe is a definite no-no? Furious, I took that moment to scream out to the crowd, "I am no goddamn Aunt Martha!" and walked away, losing every smidgen of respect I'd had for that man as a minister.

Many people came to me afterwards and apologized, saying how sorry they were that I had to bear the embarrassment and humiliation of such a statement. I was far too angry to feel humiliated. I couldn't believe an acclaimed civil rights leader could be such a racist. I couldn't believe that a man whom God had supposedly called out to help people, to lead them to a better place, would stand before such a big crowd and say something so deliberately hurtful. In my personal opinion, I think maybe God called Mr. Jackson to come out off the streets, and he misunderstood and thought God had called him to preach.

Jackson did not refer to any other white candidate as a

"no-no." There was speculation that the note had been passed to Jackson by someone who believed Joe was becoming too popular in the community and was gaining a little too much fame and trust and feared that might lead him to run for a bigger office one day, maybe even mayor. But that was simply speculation. The "Uncle Joe" was, all agreed, seen as a way to bring him down a peg or two.

The day of the election was a very tense day for me. Joe and I both knew the day would not pass without some irregularities at the polling places, especially after the speech Mr. Jackson had given the day before. We both felt expectant but were not sure exactly what we expected.

Early that morning when I went in to cast my vote, the people were already gathered around the poll booths talking, whispering, and staring. Small groups later turned into larger groups, discussing the events and Mr. Jackson's speech. Sometimes, their conversations were loud and angry-sounding, and sometimes they were whispered and hushed. In reality, many seemed torn by indecision over what was right and what was wrong.

Joe was the one who had a track record of community service and business experience. I believe the voters were trying to decide whether or not to vote for the best man or to listen to Mr. Jackson and vote black no matter what. They knew the voters carried the responsibility of doing the right thing for *all* the citizens of Jefferson County, but the election became a fierce political battle, dividing the town again, pitting blacks against blacks and blacks against whites.

At one polling place, a poll watcher for Joe said that he felt so intimidated by the opponent's watchers that he simply up and left. Another poll watcher called and reported that some representatives of the opponent's team had actually gone into the voting booths with some of the elderly people who could not read or write to mark their ballots for them. Who those people wanted to vote for wasn't important; the opponent's team chose who they thought they should vote for. In no way could those elderly people know for sure if they had voted for the candidates of their choices. When a poll worker for Joe complained about that procedure, he was ridiculed and asked to leave.

When the returns came in, Joe congratulated his opponent and offered his help in the event he ever needed it. His opponent was qualified, but not as qualified as Joe. I don't say that just because Joe is my husband. The two never did become friends, but they did develop a working relationship. That old slogan "vote for the best man" didn't apply in that election. "Vote for the black man" had become the new mantra.

The outcome of the election could have been challenged on the grounds of irregularities, but would it have been worth it? The case would have, undoubtedly, gone to a biased judge, and besides, the challenge would have only made Joe look like a sore loser. I felt Joe made the right decision to forget the whole debacle and move on. Our lives had withstood many obstacles; we didn't need any more to contend with.

The irregularities that occurred that day were not reflections on Joe's opponent's character, or his ability to do the job he was elected to do. It was not his doing but the doing of others. He probably would have won the election without the intimidation, but his workers chose to take no chances.

A much younger black man defeated the longtime circuit clerk who had held that position since 1948. The chancery clerk, who had held that position just as long, was also defeated. Those two old, crusty white men were caught by surprise. They had held those positions for so long that, I believe, they thought they would never be uprooted.

Mr. Jackson had breezed into our town for the announced purpose of conducting a rally to motivate people to vote. That rally, however, was nothing more than a drummed-up support system for blacks running for office in Jefferson County. If the focus of the rally had been to motivate voters to support the candidates they felt could have best represented the county, there would have been no need for any slandering. The real reason Mr. Jackson came to town was to get the message across to blacks to support other blacks, regardless of whether they were the most qualified or not, an outdated version of the politics of the sixties.

The election was not a black/white issue, but an issue of what was best for the citizens of Jefferson County, and Jesse Jackson's exhortations did not create an outcome that was the best one for our county. Of course, he didn't have to live in our town for the next four years, much less for the rest of his life. It was easy for him to ride in, speak for an hour and a half, and leave, never to return again.

Good black men and women were on the ballot, and once they were elected, I am sure they did their best to make our county a more progressive place for all of us to live. But good white men were also on the ballot, something Mr. Jackson couldn't have known when he cut down all whites. He should have examined all the issues and the state of affairs of the county before making such an inappropriate speech.

"We don't need more jobs; we need more positions of power!" was a most inappropriate statement to make. In a county where unemployment was currently at its highest level ever, to say that we didn't need jobs was like telling a hungry man he didn't need food.

I had welcomed Mr. Jackson into our town, because I knew he had the ability to reach all people. He had the capability to convince the voters how important it was to go to the polls and vote. However, it wasn't long before I regretted my welcome, and I resented Mr. Jackson's invasion into our tightly knit community, as well as his intrusion into Joe's and my lives. He came in and automatically assumed all control and decision-making for the town. He didn't come in and advise us; he came in and *told* us. For that moment, when he was making his speech, he took complete control of Jefferson County and the people in it.

What I found more puzzling was the unknown, inner force that had driven that man to come and speak to us as if he were a part of the election. The election itself was very exhausting, and the people's attitudes were even more frightening. We certainly didn't need the force of Jesse Jackson adding fuel to the fire.

For people like Mr. Jesse Jackson, it was still an issue of black and white. We should have been beyond that by then. It was time to look past the color of a man's skin and judge him by his merits. As long as the issue of black vs. white was hanging over us like a dark cloud, the future was going to be like the past: bleak.

11
My Children's Problems Dealing with an Interracial Marriage

We thought that, with time, things would get easier, but nothing really got easier—even the normally pleasant experiences in life can become unpleasant when you are living in an environment that does not accept you. We went to purchase a car from a local Lincoln-Ford-Mercury dealership, for example. I wanted a canary yellow Lincoln Town Car, and I was excited—couldn't wait to make the deal! I loved the look of that car. Usually when prospective buyers walk onto a lot, they are immediately met by a salesperson, sometimes more than one. As we approached the building, we could plainly see several salespeople standing around, but as we got closer, they quickly turned away—some began talking to each other, others sat down at their desks as though suddenly involved in paperwork.

I whispered to Joe about what I observed, and instead of going into the place, we turned and walked around, pretending to be looking at other cars. We had driven by the dealership several times during the week and already knew which car we wanted. The car was on display inside. We knew we needed to be inside to inspect it for ourselves. We walked around looking at other cars, waiting for someone to come out to help us. We waited a very long time. Finally, a young white salesman in his mid-thirties or so came up to us and asked, "May I help you, folks?"

"I want to purchase a car for my wife," Joe explained. "She's interested in the yellow Town Car that's showcased in your window."

The salesman looked at me and then turned back to Joe. "We have lots of good used cars here," he said in a monotone. "I could show you what we have."

"She's not interested in any other car," Joe said. "She wants to see the one in the showcase, and she'd like to test-drive it."

With an air of discomfort, he proceeded to take us inside to show us the car. I was in love with the car, but I didn't like the tire rims. I liked the ones on the 1984—the one-year-old model—better. Joe asked the salesman if we could buy the 1985 model with 1984 tire rims.

The salesman said no. He was awfully grim and taciturn for a person who was on the verge of making a big sale.

The other salespeople now moved a little closer, I guess to hear better.

"Well," Joe said, "I guess then we'll have to special order what we want." Joe told him to order me a 1985 car from the factory in Detroit with the 1984 rims and with a sun roof.

The other salespeople stared at us.

The salesman's face turned red, but he ordered the car . . . with malice. For a man who was about to make a sale, he was awfully grumpy, asking us the necessary questions without looking at us, and then hurrying us out the door.

Except for expressing my feelings about the tires, I didn't do much talking. Joe did most of the talking. He always warned me about my mouth because I was very much a fighter. He knew I was irritated and I knew I should let him handle this rather than make a sticky situation even stickier.

"I'm sorry for the way he treated you," Joe said softly on the way home. He always apologized when he felt I had been mistreated by someone white. I really wished he didn't have to keep apologizing.

The car arrived and I loved it and, admittedly, I got a kick out of the way it stood out because of its color and its customized features. I decided to take things one step further by getting a customized license plate. I wanted "Sassy" but settled for "Sazzy" since "Sassy" was already taken. One day as I was driving down the road, a car pulled up beside me at the stoplight. The white man who was driving rolled down his window and threw a cup of hot coffee at my car. At first, I didn't know what it was and was terrified until I realized it was just coffee. The light turned. He hollered out his window, "Black bitch!" and drove off. I had to pull over to the side of the road to compose myself—to remind myself that my feelings were hurt, but not my body—before I could go on. The incident killed my spirit for shopping that day, however. Instead of heading to the store, I just went back home.

The largest local department store back then was McRae's. As I was looking around the store one day, I walked over to the Clinique cosmetic counter and checked out the shades of nail polish. I liked Clinique's best because the polish seemed thicker and richer in texture. There was only one saleslady behind the counter. She was waiting on a white customer when I walked up, but there was no one else around. So, I thought when she was finished, she'd come over to me. I continued to look. The customer left and the saleslady still didn't come over. A few minutes later, another white customer walked up and she jumped at the opportunity to help her.

"Hi," she said enthusiastically as she walked over to where the lady was standing. "How may I help you today?" They proceeded with whatever the customer was buying.

After she finished with that customer, she still didn't come over to me. By now, I knew she was deliberately ignoring me, but I decided to wait her out because I knew sooner or later, she'd have to come to me. I stayed in that area an hour before that saleslady finally approached me. I had no place I needed to be, so I had plenty of time.

"May I help you today?"

I turned around and looked her in the eye and said, "No, you can't help me today, but I'm going to help you."

She looked stunned. I could plainly see the blood rushing to her face as it took on a deeper and deeper shade of red. I almost laughed because her face reminded me of the shade of the nail polish I'd wanted to buy. I didn't say anything else at first; I wanted her to stew and worry about what I was going to do or say. I continued to stare at her.

"Ma'am," she said finally, "I was just giving you time to find what you were looking for without feeling rushed."

"Couldn't you have come up with a better lie than that?" I asked her.

She stuttered, murmuring something I didn't understand. Then after all of that, she blurted out, "I didn't see you!"

Well, that took the cake. I looked her up and down. Then I asked, "Ma'am, are you tired?"

She said, "Oh no."

I said, "Ma'am, if I looked like you, I would be. With those uncomfortable-looking shoes on your feet, standing all day, I would. And with the outdated bouffant hairstyle, you look tired. Maybe this job is too much for you. Maybe you should find you something else more suitable for older, tired people like yourself." With that, I turned and walked out of the store.

As I looked back, she was still standing there with her mouth hanging open.

Joe was right about my mouth.

Gradually, these kinds of incidents just wear a person down. You walk around with a chip on your shoulder, waiting for the stares to start when you go some place as a black woman with two black children and a white husband. And there were always stares—hostile ones—and often more than stares. There were unkind remarks made, or subtle actions taken that made us even more self-conscious. They ate away at me and I'm afraid I served as a conduit, passing my anger down to my children. Nikki and Shea were becoming tense, angry teenagers with volcanic tempers, right before my eyes. I absolutely understood when they told me that they felt like fake black intruders in the black world and truly outsiders in the white world. There was racism and there was economic jealousy and they were apt targets for each. They not only had a white father, which angered both whites and blacks, but they also had a standard of living better than most. We owned a grocery store and had a big well-kept home.

"Your mama thinks she's s-o-o much," the kids spat at my girls at school.

"Your mama thinks she's white just cuz she married a white man!"

"Y'all think you're something because y'all own a store," the neighborhood kids would taunt.

Nikki—the child with attitude—would snap back, "Yes, we do. So what?"

Shea, in contrast, would usually take it all in and run to me with tears streaming down her face. My heart wept for them when I heard them talk about what was going on around them, but most of the time, I felt exactly the same way they did. No world was created in Fayette for a family like ours.

The only place they seemed to feel comfortable was with my family—their cousins. There they were accepted. Auntie Ruth's kids were their favorites and so was Auntie Ruth.

During the summers, it was hard to keep them home, as Auntie Ruth's house became a second home for them. There they could be totally black and totally accepted.

I frantically tried to explain racism to my children, but I couldn't, because I didn't particularly understand it myself. I wanted to explain their black heritage to them in such a way that they would not feel that their color was a burden to them, but rather an inheritance to be proud of. I thought that if I could instill enough black pride and self-respect in them, then they had nothing to fear from others of a different ethnicity. When I think back to those times, I now know I took their quietness for understanding.

My children were delicate little souls, absorbing everything I fed to them. I pretty much made them see the world through my eyes. I never gave them a chance to see it through their own, nor did I allow them to draw their own conclusions about issues that were important to them. Teaching my children to spot racism became my national anthem. Nikki's constant comment was, "Mom, you preach so much, you should have your own pulpit."

As the tension grew among us, I felt their belief in me as a parent was slipping away. I knew that I was trying to teach them concepts that I didn't really believe in myself, that things would be okay (but it wasn't so, really), that there would be a better day for us (but I didn't believe it), that not all people, both black and white, were prejudiced like the people in Fayette (but I certainly didn't believe that in my heart), that people in other areas of the country lived by more peaceful values (but how would I know?), that people would finally accept us (and my heart sank every time I said that; I just couldn't convince myself of that one).

Every time we went out together in public as a family, there would be some incident that would make the lectures

I'd given them at home about people in general seem to be a lie. As soon as there was some public display that caused our feelings to be hurt, I'd get so upset I'd refute all the happy platitudes I'd offered before and demonstrate my anger and hatred. It's natural for teenagers to start pulling away from family outings, but Nikki and Shea had to contend with the double whammy of not only being seen with their parents, but being seen with one black and one white parent.

Instead of teaching my children hatred and how to fight battles, I should have been teaching them how to be big and strong enough to pick and choose which battles were worth fighting. I should have told them that they would always find some obstacles in their lives, many placed on them by themselves. I did an inept job of preparing Nikki and Shea for the outside world through my own warped thinking.

They told me much later in life that they felt it was just the two of them against the whole world. I could only imagine how lonely that world must have been. Kids grow up fast under pressure, and sometimes they grow older and wiser. I watched my children grow into individuals whom I had no power to stop or control. I watched them struggle with finding their own ways to deal with the unusual family life that was placed upon them. I watched them trying to accept our lifestyle, yet at the same time fighting it.

Why hadn't I listened to Joe years before and moved to California? Many, many nights, I tossed and turned, brooding about the events in our lives. One night in particular, the rain began to fall, the lightning knifed through the heavy clouds, and the sky opened up and dumped buckets down on the town. The heavy downpour seemed to beat in tune to my thoughts as confirmation of what was going on my life. While the storm raged outside, my heart raged just as vigorously inside.

Nikki became an avid reader, and her enthusiasm for reading was very welcoming because books gave her a temporary escape from her everyday problems. She spent hours reading in her room, and every time we went to a mall, she made a mad dash for the bookstore. If I was shopping for something for her, and she needed to try it on, I'd have to go to the bookstore to retrieve her.

By the time Nikki turned fourteen, she had taken on that "I don't care" attitude. She made up her mind that no one cared for her; therefore, she would care for no one.

Nikki felt that I loved Shea more than I did her. Nothing I said or did seemed to change her mind. She wanted to have a dog for a pet so that she could have something of her very own. I thought it was a good idea, because having an animal around her that she loved and wanted to protect might give her some inkling of how I felt as a parent. We searched until we finally found just the right dog and presented it to her for a birthday present. She immediately fell in love with her dog and gave her all of her attention. We bought a dog collar and let her decide what name to have engraved on it.

She went through many names before deciding on Ginger Ann Rossignol. I noticed that she gave Ginger the same last name that the rest of us had, which kind of surprised me since she wasn't too fond of using it herself. She saved all of her allowance to buy gifts for Ginger. She bought all colors of sweaters for the cold winter months, and Ginger pranced around proudly wearing them.

It was very easy to see the loving side of Nikki when she was around Ginger. Her fondness showed through in the way she handled her and took care of her. Ginger was no special breed, just a mutt, but that didn't stop Nikki from loving her any less.

Ginger became like a third child for Joe and me, and Nikki's very own baby. We celebrated Ginger's birthdays with special treats, took pictures of her and with her. She went on trips with us, during which she always made it known that she wasn't going to stay in the car. We all grew to love Ginger as much as Nikki did.

I thought that by using Ginger as an example, I could explain to Nikki about love. One day, I asked her if she had two pets and one was loving, kind, and was always licking her face, and the other one was mean, ferocious, and constantly biting her hand, which one would she favor the most. She looked up at me rather suspiciously at first and said, "The one that was loving and kind and licked my face all the time."

I took that opportunity to try to explain my feelings about her and Shea. I told her that she pulled away from me all the time while Shea moved towards me. It was not that I loved Shea more, it was just that Shea gave me fewer problems, and in turn, I favored her more. I told her that I loved them both very much; I just loved them differently. I was hoping that she could understand my love for her more after having grown to love Ginger so deeply.

Silent tears, mixed with laughter, devastation, and hope, all at the same time, these were my everyday emotions. I cried more on the inside than the outside, because I was too full of pride to let my inner self be seen. I knew I had done something to hurt my children by imposing an interracial marriage on them. On the outside, though, I tried to lead as normal a life as I could. I came to believe that much of what Nikki and Shea lived through and experienced was, indeed, my fault, but I was so in love with my husband I chose not to do anything about it.

The burning pain that roared in the pit of my stomach branched out into my shoulders and neck, and the anguish throbbed, like a hard rubber mallet hitting an iron anvil. Every time I had to leave my house, I just knew I'd be unlucky enough to see someone who was surely going to treat me in some way that would cause the burning knot in my stomach to grow larger and that throbbing pain in my shoulders to become fiercer. Lying in bed at night, I'd ask myself, "Would you do anything differently if you had it to do all over again?" I couldn't imagine living without Joe. During my darkest moments, my mind would be whirling and howling for answers, just like the wind outside, but the wind would cease, and my mind would keep on going until I fell asleep, exhausted.

Even though Lee ceased to be in the girls' lives, I would, once in a while, take them to see their paternal grandparents. But when Nikki was fourteen and Shea twelve, I received a call late one night from Nikki to come pick them up. One of Lee's brothers had done the unthinkable. He had exposed himself to them. When I heard that, I rushed out to pick them up, and after that incident I never allowed them to go back.

We finally decided to send the girls away to boarding school. We made this decision based on several things; we wanted them to experience something other than what our town had to offer; we wanted them to realize how important getting a good education was to their future lives; and we wanted them to know that there was a whole new world out there, beyond the one they were growing up in, a world where people of all creeds and colors got along.

We tried to choose a school that was as close to home as possible, but the ones we looked at in Mississippi did not meet our objectives. We finally found one that we both liked in Atchinson, Kansas, the Academy of Mt. Saint Scholastica. It wasn't close to home, but I liked the campus and the atmosphere—the fact that there were many students of different races and cultures. We met with the school officials and teachers and felt very comfortable with them. They answered all of our concerns and made us feel that our children would be very welcome at their school.

I will never forget the day we left home in August 1984 to make the long drive to Kansas. That was probably one of the quietest drives we'd ever made. Nikki was fifteen, and Shea was thirteen. Rather than seeing it as an opportunity of meeting different people and being exposed to different cultures, Nikki felt she was being punished for her rebellious behavior. Shea didn't understand why her mother and father were making her go away from home. The fact that the car was loaded with personal belongings and special mementos to help them feel comfortable meant nothing. Joe and I talked, in general, but the kids were sullen, withdrawn, and had next to nothing to say. They sat quietly in the back seat staring out of the window, each lost in her own thoughts. Even when I tried to make conversation with them, they hardly responded.

This would be the first time they had ever left home for a long period of time without me. Joe and I tried to ease their fears about their new surroundings. We wanted them to know that we were only a plane ride away if they ever needed us for anything. We let them know that we would all spend all holidays together, whether it was in Kansas, Mississippi, or someplace else. I wanted to give them all the assurance I possibly could.

I was beginning to feel that I had finally outgrown my hometown, a place I once thought I would never leave. My entire family, except for my brother, still lived there. Would I be able to walk away from all of them to try something new and different? Joe and I had many long talks before I was able to finally say, a year after the talks began, "Yes, yes, let's move."

In November of 1985, we moved to Jackson, Mississippi, having decided on Jackson because it was still relatively close to home. I could drive the seventy-five miles to see my family from time to time. It was also big enough that we wouldn't be so noticeable if we just kept to ourselves. We didn't know anyone there to speak of, although my friend Macy Talbot had moved there a few years back, so keeping our lives private would be relatively easy. At the same time, Jackson provided a refreshing change from the small town atmosphere that we were leaving behind.

Once we moved away, I started to grow more and more as a person. Exploring life away from Fayette was like a breath of fresh air. I hadn't realized that the town had grown on me like a fungus and that this would mark the start of a long, healing process.

We finally sold the business back to Mr. Smith, and Joe went to work for him as a supervisor managing the other New Deal chain of stores. He was also still managing the store in Fayette on a part-time basis. It seemed like we had the best of both worlds, Fayette and Jackson.

Although we had moved away from all the injustices that had disturbed me the most while living back home, I still had a kind of restlessness about my life. I needed more. I liked living in Jackson, but I had the urge to continue to explore. Once I had a taste of something different, I felt the need to continue searching.

In spite of our broader surroundings, whenever Joe and I ventured out together, we were still stared at as if we were aliens. Sometimes, it was hard to distinguish the looks we received, whether they were looks of hatred or looks of curiosity. If we went out for dinner, we were always asked the same question, "Separate check?" I thought our demeanor showed that we were much more than mere acquaintances.

I was the only black person that lived on our street in Jackson. During the winters, someone was always coming by selling firewood. One day the doorbell rang and I was upstairs doing something, but our house had an intercom system installed. I pushed the button and asked, "Who is it?"

"Ma'am," the voice said, "I am selling firewood and wanted to know if you'd be interested in buying some."

"Just a minute," I replied. "I'll be right down." Joe and I usually bought quite a bit of firewood at the beginning of the winter because we used our fireplace a lot. Winters in Mississippi can be very cold. I went downstairs, opened the door hoping to have a look at the wood before committing to buying any. A black man was standing there, and I smiled and said, "Hi."

"Is, ah, the lady of the house home?" he asked.

I realized immediately he was thinking I had to be the maid. "No, she's not home," I told him.

"What time will she be back?"

I said, "I'm not sure, but I'll let her know you came by."

He thanked me and strolled off. A few days later, the same man came back again and asked whether the lady of the house was home; and again I said, "No, she's not home" and closed the door before he could say anything else.

A few days later I was getting ready to go out and went to the back of the house, got in my car and let the garage door up. There was the wood man standing in my driveway. I got out of the car and asked, "May I help you?"

He looked a little surprised and asked, "Ma'am, are *you* the lady of the house?"

I said, "Yes, but I don't need any of your wood."

Joe and I laughed about that one.

A year after moving to Jackson, we bought a house and I joined the neighborhood garden club, thinking this would be a good way to meet new people. During the holidays, the garden club committee usually gave a big Christmas party. That year the party was held at the president of the committee's house. This was one of the functions they put on for all of its members for the holiday season. I was excited about getting dressed up and attending the party, for Christmas was one of my favorite times of the year.

I knew most of the women who would be there but had met very few of the husbands. Joe and I left for the party all dressed up, looking forward to having a good time. When we arrived at the party, it was in full bloom with much laughing and folks milling around talking. Some were in large groups, while others gathered in smaller groups, but they all had glasses in their hands ready to propose a toast to any occasion.

I introduced Joe to the hostess, and though she tried to be very cool, I noticed her eyebrows arching in surprise as she shook his hand. We picked up some drinks and joined the crowd, mingling and saying hello here and there. I was the only black woman, so most assumed there must be a black man somewhere. After I introduced Joe to the hostess, we split up to mingle and grab a bite to eat. A man walked up to me, introduced himself, and said, "Martha, how are you, and where is your husband tonight?" He went on to say, "I have looked everywhere, and I don't see him anywhere."

I wanted to asked why was he looking for him so hard but I responded with, "He's around here somewhere."

About a half hour later, that same man came up to me again and said he never found my husband. I looked around the room and spotted Joe's back turned to me and told the man that he was right over there, talking to a group of men. He looked over at the group that I was staring at and asked, "Which one is your husband?"

I pointed him out, describing him as "the guy with the red hair."

He turned as red as Joe's hair, mumbling something as he backed away. He wasted no time in telling some of the others at the party who my husband was. Everyone did stay pretty cool about it, but I would have had to have been blind not to notice the extra stares and the lowering of the eyes whenever Joe and I were near.

There had to be a place where interracial marriages were more accepted. California came up yet again, but I just wasn't too keen on moving that far away from both Fayette and the girls' school. It was such a huge state, and at heart, I've always been a small-town gal.

I definitely don't want to give the impression that all experiences with white people were bad. My longtime friend Bob and her husband had just adopted a baby girl, and I went shopping one day to find something special to send them to celebrate their happiness. While I was shopping in a baby store in Jackson, Small Fry, the saleslady asked if she could help me find something. When I told her about my friend's baby, she told me about another woman who was in the store at that very same moment, buying a gift for her and her husband's newly adopted baby girl. I didn't talk to the adoptive mother, but the saleslady told me that she and her mother had driven over from Meridian, Mississippi, and were shopping together for the new addition to their family. The adoptive mother was white.

I found what I was looking for, had it gift-wrapped, and then asked the saleslady to gift-wrap another item I had picked out to give to the other adoptive parent, anonymously. I asked that she please wait until I'd left the store before giving her the gift. The saleslady did so, but I found out later that she also gave the woman my name and address. About a week later, I received a "thank you" note from the white woman, whose name I learned was Lori Bush, along with a picture of their new baby girl, Katie. We have been writing to each other ever since, exchanging Christmas cards, and I send birthday cards to her daughter and son, David, whom they adopted a few years later. I receive updated pictures of the children and school information concerning them. I have never personally met the family, but we've been in touch for close to twenty years now.

This experience came at a time in my life when I was becoming ever-so-consumed with hatred and trying not to hate all white people at the same time. I'm grateful that something told me to "take a chance . . . see what happens."

By 1989, I had become consumed by racism and hatred. This was a complete turnaround from the sunny outlook of a little girl who spent her childhood in an isolated familial cocoon blissfully ignorant of racial prejudice. The hatred that had increasingly built up inside me was, no doubt, fed in large part by the way Joe and I were still treated as an interracial couple.

I knew it was time to leave Mississippi when I felt I was losing touch with myself, losing the parts of me I liked best: my self-esteem, my spirit, and my cheerful outlook on life in general.

I started talking to Joe about moving away; maybe now the time had finally come for us to put Mississippi behind us altogether. I felt I was ready to shed the past and try to focus on a new life in a new place.

Looking in an employment ad, I found that place: Bermuda. We sold the house in Fayette and our house in Jackson and made a clean break. I even sold my canary yellow Lincoln that I'd dreamed of owning for so many years.

12
Hello, Bermuda ... Goodbye, Racism

Our move to Bermuda actually started out as a joke. While thumbing through the classified section in a trade magazine called *Supermarket News*, I saw an ad for a job listed in Bermuda. Joe had been looking at other ads, but the possibility of living in Bermuda was more appealing.

Joe sent out resumes to several companies. I typed up a cover letter and sent it along with his resume to the Bermuda address without his knowledge. I thought it couldn't do any harm, and besides, we probably wouldn't hear back from them anyway. I didn't tell Joe what I had done until three days later as we talked about other job possibilities.

The following Saturday, a man called and asked to speak with Joe. I told him that Joe was at work and offered to take a message for him. My goddaughter, Heather, whom I was keeping for the weekend, began to fuss just as the call came in. I picked her up and juggled the phone as best as I could while trying to speak calmly to the voice on the other end. The man said he was calling from Bermuda.

I almost dropped the phone. Was I ever surprised to be receiving a call only a week after I'd mailed the resume and letter! At that moment, my goddaughter began to cry loudly into the phone. The man immediately wanted to know whose baby was crying, since it was stated in the cover letter that both our kids were grown and living on their own. I explained that she was our godchild, and we were just keeping her for the weekend, which seemed to satisfy him. We made small talk, and he asked for a number where Joe could be reached during the day, followed by a few more questions, and then we hung up.

I was so excited I could hardly do anything for the rest of the day except wait for Joe to come home. I played with Heather and chattered with her, telling her all about our hopes to go to Bermuda, as if she could understand a word I was saying. She was only three months old, but if someone had heard me talking to her, I swear they would have thought I was talking to a much older person.

I kept watching for Joe to come home and was waiting by the door when he finally walked in. I wanted to know all about the conversation he'd had on the phone with the man from Bermuda. I wanted to know everything they talked about, every detail. He tried to repeat the conversation to me as he remembered it. A good memory has never been one of Joe's strongest suits. That job was the main topic of conversation in our house for the next few days, because it looked like we might be headed for an unknown adventure.

In April 1989, the company called to tell us that they had made arrangements to have us flown to Bermuda for two nights and three days. The first day Joe was to have an interview, and the other two days we'd have some free time. We decided to make the trip a week long and pay for the remainder of the days ourselves since we had never visited Bermuda before.

Bermuda's serene beauty came as a pleasant surprise to me. The population was a little over fifty thousand. There was no illiteracy to speak of, as far as I could tell, no unemployment, no poverty, and no income tax. Hamilton, the capital, was also the largest city on the island. Front Street was the main thoroughfare and where all the main attractions were, where the cruise ships docked, where shoppers and browsers enjoyed the quaint shops and quality goods.

The brilliant colors of the setting sun illuminated the peaceful beauty of the island, which was one of the world's most isolated inhabited islands. The characteristic pastel-colored houses, surrounded by brilliant flowers, gave the landscape a picturesque look.

We had a great time exploring. By the end of that week, I knew Joe's mind was made up. He told me that if he was offered a job, then he was going to take it and would like my support. He also confided that one of his lifelong dreams had been to live on an island. It was a dream he had never shared with me up until that time. The employer told us before we left that he would get back to us in a few days. The feeling was positive; we did get the call. It looked like we were headed to Bermuda!

Now the time had come for us to tell our children and our families of our plans. We thought it best to tell Nikki and Shea first, stressing to them that they would be coming for visits and all holidays.

My sisters showed concern when they heard the news but actually took it rather well. I'm sure they knew we had made up our minds by the determined way we told them. We gave them the same opportunity as with the kids—the invitation to come and visit whenever they liked. We relayed as much information about Bermuda as was given to us, which wasn't much, but it did seem to ease their concerns somewhat.

We were told to pick up whatever items we thought we might need before moving, because most things were almost twice the price they would be in the United States. A good pair of walking shoes was a must, as walking was considered a form of transportation on the island.

Joe went to the mall alone to buy himself a good comfortable pair, while I stayed home packing. When he returned, he told me I should go to the same store he had, because he'd noticed there was a good selection of both men's and women's shoes. In the middle of packing the next day, I stopped and took a break to run over to the mall to have a look.

As we walked into the store, the girl behind the counter took one look at us and immediately picked up the telephone, dialed a number, and started talking. The other salesperson was waiting on a customer. We proceeded to look around at the different shoes, trying to be patient as we waited for one of the two salesclerks to help us.

The girl behind the counter was still on the phone, and the guy was still waiting on the previous customer. A short time later, a white customer walked in. The girl on the phone hung up just as abruptly as she had picked it up when we walked in. She immediately turned her attention to the new customer and asked in a very pleasant voice, "May I help you find something today?"

Here we go again. Joe whispered to me to stay calm and continue to look around. By now, I was really irritated, but I did listen to him. If I hadn't needed those shoes I would have walked out.

After that last customer left, the girl finally came up to us and said in an overly friendly voice, "Have you found what you need?"

I turned, looked at her, and asked, "How long did you think it would take us to find what we needed?" She looked embarrassed and made no comment.

Joe commented that when he'd been in the store alone the day before he'd been waited on immediately.

At first, I was angry. But after seeing how uncomfortable

she was, I suddenly wanted to laugh in her face. I selected the shoes I wanted, paid for them, and left.

At the end of April, I flew back to Bermuda for another week to look for housing. We called and made all the necessary arrangements through a real estate agency for me to meet a Reverend Malcolm Eve, the person who would be showing me a house he had for rent. He told me on the phone that he would be responsible for finding me a place to stay while I was there. I stayed with the Jacob family, and I thoroughly enjoyed my time there. Later, we would become good friends with the Jacobs and their entire clan.

I was picked up from the airport by Reverend Eve, a Bermudian Methodist minister. He had traveled quite a bit in the United States doing missionary work for other churches. He was a handsome, distinguished-looking man, well dressed, and quite well spoken. He had a pleasant, welcoming manner about him that I found to be true of many Bermudians.

The house we were supposed to rent was right behind the Jacobs' house. It was high upon a hill overlooking the ocean with breathtaking views. When Reverend Eve and I arrived at the Jacobs' house, only Mr. Jacob was home. I was introduced to him, and his warm manner immediately made me feel welcome. Standing out on the deck, I could feel the wind blowing through the palm and banana trees in their front yard. The flowers in Bermuda were in full bloom with the scents emphasized by the ocean breeze.

Mr. Jacob showed me to the room where I'd be sleeping and the bath where I could freshen up. I wasn't at all tired from the trip over, and as a matter of fact, I felt it was going to be useless trying to get any sleep that night. I made a quick trip to the washroom, washed my face, and went back out to the kitchen, because I didn't want to miss anything. So far, everything about my trip was overwhelming: the people, the serenity, the atmosphere, and the quietness of the island.

I almost had to pinch myself; here I was, a small-town girl from the Deep South looking for a place to stay in one of the world's most beautiful vacation spots. Reverend Eve, Mr. Jacob, and I were sitting around the kitchen table chatting when a tall, beautiful Bermudian woman walked in. Mr. Jacob stood and introduced her as his wife, Olga. I knew once we moved, I'd be very happy around this woman. She immediately put me at ease with her affectionate ways.

Bermudians speak in a soft, lilting mixture of British and American English. That was forged, no doubt, by Bermuda's status as a British colony and its relatively close proximity to the United States for travel and tourism.

As it worked out, I didn't rent the house behind the Jacobs, but Joe and I did come to know them very well. They became our family away from home. Most people don't have the opportunity to choose a family, but I was fortunate. Mama Jacob and Dad Jacob became Joe's and my adopted parents by our own choosing.

Although the location of the rental house was perfect in setting, the decor wasn't to my liking. I couldn't get past the color scheme. I called the real estate agent to help me locate another place as I didn't want my trip to be a complete waste of time. The agent's name was Frederick Beach. We became very good friends and remained so until his death. He told me about an apartment building that was being built, which should be finished by the time Joe and I moved there to live. He said he felt I would be very pleased with it, because he had seen the plans, and it was to be beautifully constructed.

The site was just a piece of land to me, but the views were awesome. The complex was going to be situated on a narrow strip of land with ocean views in front and back. Standing on that hill looking out gave me a very calm and peaceful feeling. I rented an apartment in the to-be-constructed complex.

When I arrived home, I was excited and full of details about my findings. I wanted to give Joe every account of my weeklong visit. In the middle of the night, I found myself thinking of some small matter that I'd forgotten to mention, which promptly made me wake Joe up to tell him. He is a very deep sleeper and didn't appreciate these interruptions at all. His usual grumpy response was, "Couldn't it have waited until morning?"

Joe and I made our big move on June 3, 1989. We were both excited about our new life, but also were beset with fears of the unknown, I probably more so than Joe, as he had lived in other places: Connecticut, New York, California, Iowa, and, of course, Mississippi.

On the way to Bermuda, I had many thoughts going around in my head. Before landing, we circled that little fishhook-shaped island twice, and from the air, everything looked picture perfect; the lush green foliage and stretches of pink coral beaches were outstanding features. The landscape was unique and romantic.

The pilot announced that the temperature was in the mid-eighties with no overcast. It was a calm, beautiful day, and I could hardly wait to land. Once cleared through customs, Joe and I were ready to start our new life.

Mr. Beach met us at the airport and drove us to see our new home. He played tour guide for us as well, pointing out the many different points of interest. Joe and I gazed out the window, each lost in our own thoughts.

When Mr. Beach pulled up at the apartment complex

where we were to live, I became more than a little worried. The building was still in the process of being built. The construction had obviously started, but the building wasn't nearly complete enough for us to move in. The downstairs was practically finished, but the upstairs had a ways to go. Joe and I were very upset about the misleading news. We had already shipped a container load of furniture a week ahead of us, and it was supposed to arrive the following week. Mr. Beach assured us that the apartment would be finished enough to store the furniture, although we wouldn't be able to move in ourselves. He told us that he had made arrangements with the Jacobs for us to stay with them until our apartment was ready.

I met many people through my friendship with Mama Jacob. She truly did help make our move and adjustment much easier. Thanks to her, I was treated almost as a local in no time at all. I learned quite a bit from Mama Jacob and went everywhere with her, to the post office, the grocery store, and even to some of her senior citizen meetings. Through her, I also experienced the different taste of Bermudian foods.

On Good Friday, the kitchens of Bermuda's homes were bathed in the aroma of freshly baked hot cross buns and codfish cakes. At Christmas, the traditional dish was cassava pie, and on Guy Fawkes Day, November 5, it was sweet potato pudding.

Sunday morning breakfast consisted of codfish and potatoes—a delicious combination of salt cod and boiled potatoes garnished with hard-boiled eggs, bananas, avocado pear, and a tangy tomato sauce made with tomatoes, garlic, onions, and green peppers. Those dishes were served up with a good helping of love well-seasoned fun with a dash of southern charm.

I was continually amazed by the nice gestures and the totally calm way Bermudians went about everyday life. Their laid-back culture was just what I needed in order to take a good, long look at Joe's and my life together, the lives of my children, how I had allowed the attitudes of others to affect my own life, and how my own attitude had spilled out to others. The peace and the serenity were more than fulfilling.

Vincent, who was helping to complete the work on our apartment, asked if I'd like to go fishing. I told him yes, but I didn't have any fishing gear. He said not to worry; he had everything I needed.

Fishing in Bermuda, as I soon found out, was quite different from any fishing I had ever done. Vincent didn't have a fishing pole or a reel. He had nothing that I could see to make me think we were about to go fishing. I wanted to ask questions but thought I should stay quiet. I was thinking, "Maybe this is how they do it here," but fishing is fishing; how many ways can it be done?

We walked down to the ocean, with me doing most of the talking; Vincent was a very quiet person. When we got to the spot where we were going to fish, he proceeded to unwind this thick string he pulled out of his pocket. He then put a large hook on the end of it. He assembled one for me as well. I was puzzled, wondering what we were going to do with this string! Seeing my puzzled look, he told me we were going to catch minnows first to use for bait. He showed me how to throw the string out into the water while holding one end to pull back when something grabbed it. That was easy.

When he was satisfied with the amount of smaller fish we had caught, he then baited our hooks for the big catch. He said to throw the string as far as I could and wrap the end I was holding around a chunk of coral so the future catch wouldn't pull it into the water. He also put an empty can on the string to make a noise every time there was a nibble on it. All we had to do was sit, watch, and listen. I found that all very amusing and extremely different. I must say I did have my doubts as to how that was going to work.

About ten minutes after I had thrown my string out, something was nibbling on it. I could hear the can rattling and see the string running from side to side. I started jumping up and down, for my string was moving ferociously. I told Vincent that it had to be something really big *more like an alligator or a huge shark,* and I didn't want it. He ran over, grabbed the string, and started pulling it out of the water, running with it from side to side. I was yelling to him, "No, cut the string and let it go!" From the way it was pulling, I was petrified of what we would find on the other end.

He ignored my warnings, never letting go as he wrestled with whatever was on the other end. I stood looking on, horrified. He continued wrestling until he had pulled enough of it out of the water that a head was visible. Once I saw the head, I felt a little more relaxed and safe because I could clearly see it was a fish. I tried to help by wrapping the loose string around a big rock as he pulled. I had never seen a fish that size close up before.

The fish was so heavy, my fishing partner carried it home for me. I excitedly burst into the house, hollering for Joe to come see my catch. He took pictures of me holding the fish, and after it was cleaned, we invited a few people we had met over and had a cookout to celebrate. It was a magical night, the first time I had invited company to our place in Bermuda.

Bermuda proved to be a turning point in my life.

The end of a perfect day in Bermuda to me was dining at a local restaurant while sitting under a lovely terrace under a twinkling sky or indoors with candlelight bouncing across century-old cedar beams or taking short motorbike rides to one of the beautiful beaches for a midnight stroll in the pink sand. There's something magical about quietly walking along a deserted beach at midnight or even at sunset. Kicking off your shoes, rolling up your trousers, and wading in the water, knee deep, was an experience that could be repeated many times, but each time had a different sensation about it.

But it was much more than the physical beauty that changed me. Bermudians were a rare breed. For the most part, the island's population was a fairly tight-knit group made up of a multitude of nationalities. Joe and I no longer stuck out like a sore thumb. Interracial marriages were frequent and accepted . . . we were just another couple.

For the first time in our married life *we could be* just another couple. About two months after I arrived in Bermuda, I was hired at my first temp job at a software company, where I worked for six months, performing various and sundry tasks. I didn't resign, nor was I fired. I had to leave because my employment was terminated by the immigration department. Their laws mandated that a foreign temporary employee could only stay on the same job for six months unless it was a special assignment.

Working at the software company was a wonderful experience, and I thoroughly enjoyed the people I met there. On my last day of work, nine of the women and my boss took me out to a beautiful restaurant for a farewell lunch. Five of those ladies are still my friends today—Diane, Orreann, Beverly, Glenda, and Kim. When I met those ladies, they were all strangers to me, and just six months later, they had become very dear to me. They made me feel special, telling me how much they were going to miss me. Knowing how much I enjoyed wine, they presented me with a beautiful crystal wine decanter and a precious card with all of their names and good luck messages on it. I still have that decanter and the card to this day. It was a very touching moment, one that I will cherish forever.

The most essential key to enjoying the island was to relax and succumb to the slow, leisurely, and laid-back lifestyle of the islanders. The peacefulness was so different from the life I had led in the U.S. I felt as though I had been running for a very long time and was finally able to walk, and to walk slowly at that. I had been on a treadmill for the past fifteen years and now I had finally gotten off.

As I traveled east or west to the shores of the island while driving around, I enjoyed the verdant marshes, the sparkling beaches, and the colorful homes that were nestled behind oleander shrubs or morning glories or hibiscus trees. I learned not to be startled by the tooting of horns for that too was just an expression of hospitality or an exchange of greetings.

Living in that atmosphere gave Joe and me the opportunity to look back and reflect on our lives, to think about us and not society, to focus on our relationship. I no longer felt that when I went out in public I would be stared at with hatred or whispered about or just plain ignored. My life felt more lighthearted. I no longer felt that burden of prejudice, the need to always have my guard up. I learned to talk to white people without thinking there had to be a motive behind their wanting to talk to me. I learned how to trust, and many of those white people I met back in 1989 became lifelong friends. In fact, the biggest lesson I learned while living in Bermuda was trust. I learned that color had nothing, absolutely nothing, to do with one's character. I learned how to trust people based on my experiences with them, no matter their color. I learned that to have a good friend, one had to know how to be one. I learned how to love instead of how to hate. I was finally able to look at racism for what it was and still is—ignorance and fear.

Throughout Joe's and my years together in Mississippi we had lived in an atmosphere of tension caused by outside pressures . . . but *intensified* by our own gradual susceptibility to those pressures. I realized how sensitized I had become over the years, how aware of every slight and how vulnerable. I forced myself to stop obsessing about hurtful racist incidents I had experienced. I began to understand how the trauma of racism had put a very heavy chip on my shoulder, and I felt ready for the first time to nudge that chip off. Instead of spending time generalizing about people and situations and continually staying stuck in the past, I began to look forward to the future, to spending some time exploring my inner self.

I do believe that our life's paths are chosen for us and Bermuda was, undoubtedly, on my path and it was one that led to a complete healing process. Would our lives have been different if we'd found Bermuda when Joe and I got married? Would my daughters have had an easier time blending in to the island's multiracial mix than they'd had in Mississippi? Undoubtedly. But Bermuda had not been on our path back then. Perhaps we needed to experience what we did in order to triumph over prejudice in the end. That is what I feel I did.

Ironically, this soul searching enabled me, eventually, to go home again to visit and to enjoy my family and my birthplace. Instead of remembering Mississippi as a hateful place, I was gradually able to appreciate it for the beautiful state it is. I could enjoy the scenery, the wildflowers, and especially the sunflowers that seemed to grow wild all over the place.

I could enjoy the rich soil, the forests that cover more than half of the state, and animal and plant life. Everything had a new look about it.

If we each honestly asked ourselves as Americans, "Am I prejudiced?" and persistently kept asking that question, we would arrive at the conclusion that prejudice is inevitable by the nature of our society. Only through that self-realization will we be able to learn how to deal with this plague that swept the country historically and still prevails. I have found my peace and will continue to help others find theirs.

My life has taken many twists and turns and has been full of surprises, some good and some bad. I can say I have learned plenty over the years and have met many people from all walks of life. Life has taught me many, many lessons. One in particaular I will never forget is to always walk with my eyes wide open, not half open or half shut, but wide open. I have found that is the key that works for me.

My triumph over prejudice was what transcended me to where I am today and will continue to see me through. Racism will always have an effect upon my life, or on any black person's life for that matter, but how I allow it to affect my life will be up to me. What makes a difference in my life? It's not about the things or the people around me, but the things and people I surround myself with. I choose to live a serene lifestyle, for it gives me a chance to finish a project I started some years back: my life's story. I believe I have earned the right to associate with those people with whom I feel most comfortable. Color is no longer a factor.

As you, the reader, walked through my life with me, I hope you found your own path and will live each day of your existence on this earth to the fullest.

Figure 8. Joe and Martha